# Sizzlin' Suppers

THE EL PASO CHILE COMPANY'S

# Sizzlin' Suppers

W. PARK KERR

WILLIAM MORROW AND COMPANY, INC.
NEW YORK

Library of Congress Cataloging-in-Publication Data

Kerr, W. Park.
    The El Paso Chile Company's sizzlin' suppers / W. Park Kerr. — 1st
ed.
      p.    cm.
    Includes index.
    ISBN 0-688-13250-2
    1. Cookery, American—Southwestern style.    I. El Paso Chile
Company.    II. Title.
TX715.2.S69K47 1998
641.5979—dc21                        98-11190
                                        CIP

Printed in the United States of America

First Edition

1  2  3  4  5  6  7  8  9  10

BOOK DESIGN BY NICK ANDERSON

www.williammorrow.com

## ACKNOWLEDGMENTS

I THINK THAT WRITING A COOKBOOK IS LIKE HAVING FRIENDS OVER FOR SUPPER: IF YOU surround yourself with people you like and involve them with good food, something special is sure to come of it.

So this cookbook was created by people who I would love to see around a big dinner table someday (and maybe we all will be if we can manage to be in the same place at the same time). In the kitchen, Rick Rodgers helped me simmer up these recipes, sometimes taking just a glimmer of an idea and working it into a full-blown dish. Rick's assistant, Dianne Kniss, kept track of our faxes and phone calls and grocery bills. Rick and I both want to thank Betty Hughes at Weber-Stephens Products for the beautiful gas grill we used for recipe tasting.

Justin Schwartz, my brilliant editor at William Morrow, headed up a great team to get the manuscript between covers. Lisa Haney's illustrations have a sense of humor that I apply to my life in and out of the kitchen. Nick Anderson designed the book, and Carole Berglie was our attentive copy editor.

And no supper at my house would be complete without my wife, Martina, and our son, Grayson.

# CONTENTS

TO ME, SUPPER IS DIFFERENT FROM DINNER. DINNER IS A MEAL, BUT SUPPER IS A FRAME OF

mind. A butler in a movie would never say, "Supper is served."

Dinner is eating. Supper is therapy. Everything about supper is relaxed and relaxing.

You go out with your boss for dinner, not for supper. You never have to "dress" for supper. You

can eat supper in your sweatpants and socks and be perfectly fine.

Supper is not restaurant food. When you have guests over for a special dinner, you

might attempt chefs' recipes from cooking magazines with names like "Grilled Whachama-

callit and Whoozits on Somethingorother Coulis," and not mind washing a few extra pots and pans. But for supper you don't want a challenge. Most of the time, supper is composed from recipes that are in your head, like meat loaf and mashed potatoes. You never have to show off your culinary skills at supper. You just make good food that makes you feel good.

Supper is stew, not ragout. It's gravy or salsa, and never coulis (but every now and then it can be sauce). It loves dishes that are hot from the oven, one-pot meals, stir-fries to spoon over rice or noodles, food that is topped with crumbs, food to serve with mashed potatoes, food that fills the house with delicious aromas. Supper means food that you eat with your fingers, and you get to lick your fingers afterwards. Supper never met a finger bowl in its life.

At my house, no one is allowed to count calories at supper—save the low-fat meals for another time. That doesn't mean that we ignore healthful eating. However, there is a calculation that many health-care professionals use, suggesting that people eat healthfully 70 percent of the time, and allow themselves to get what they like the other times. These recipes are for the 30 percent of your life when you get to enjoy what is on your plate, not think about it.

Sometimes supper is thrown together in a hurry. There are plenty of recipes here that can be cooked against the clock for weeknight meals. On the other hand, supper is often prepared at leisure during the weekend. I have to admit that those are my favorite kinds of suppers, featuring long-simmered foods and special desserts.

You can have your friends over for supper, of course, but only good friends who won't talk about anything that could upset the mellow mood. And supper is a great time to get friends into the kitchen to help cook the meal. If your guests do want to talk about their problems, get them to peel carrots—working with the hands is very therapeutic.

This book is filled with recipes that I make for supper. Usually, I make supper for my wife and young son. Even if dinner is just for the three of us, I often make extra servings to act as leftovers for tomorrow's lunch or supper. (Supper loves to be turned into leftovers.)

*Sizzlin' Suppers* is about spicing up old favorites. Readers familiar with my previous books know that I love Southwestern flavors. In this book, I have branched out to include other tastes that I enjoy, too. You'll find food with Asian, Middle Eastern, Italian, and other ethnic accents. Still, many a recipe has been enlivened with a jolt of chile peppers—chipotles, jalapeños, dried New Mexico chiles all make an appearance. If chiles aren't a part of your daily life, as they are mine, they are easy to obtain. Most supermarkets these days have an increasingly large selection of Southwestern products. And what you can't get at the market, you can mail-order. I'm not asking you to mail-order just one jar of mole sauce at a time. You should think ahead and get a large order of assorted canned and bottled condiments and dried chiles for your pantry. Once you have them on hand, you will learn to rely on them as I have, zapping old-fashioned dishes with a new attitude.

# Sizzlin' Suppers

# side-dish and main-course salads

WHEN PLANNING SUPPER, DON'T LET SALADS BE AN AFTERTHOUGHT. COOL AND CRISP, their refreshing texture sets the stage for the meal. Sometimes salad *is* the meal. During one of our infamous Texas hot spells, we'll make supper out of pasta salad, served on the patio.

Of course, there's more to salads than lettuce and pasta. Potato salads, cole slaws, bean salads, salads made from one or two vegetables—how can you pick a favorite? Some salads taste better with certain foods. For example, barbecued ribs and slaw, grilled steak and potato salad, pasta with a green salad and vinaigrette. Serving cole slaw with pasta doesn't ring any bells in my book.

Every house needs a house dressing, a secret concoction that is so good that your guests ask for the recipe. There are a number of candidates for the Best House Dressing award here, from a thick blue cheese masterpiece to a simple chile-lime vinaigrette. While I have given serving suggestions for each dressing, use any greens you wish. Store any leftover dressing in a closed container in the refrigerator for up to one week.

Classically, vinaigrettes are whisked in a bowl. If you like thick vinaigrette dressings, make them in a blender. Blend the vinegar and seasonings together first, then gradually add the oil. (The blender emulsifies the mixtures better than a whisk, and it will separate upon standing, but it can be blended again before serving.)

You can toss these dressings with greens, but you'll get more servings if they are served on the side so guests can add the amount they prefer. (You may even have some leftover dressing that way.) Some of the thicker dressings should be spooned over firm-textured greens; they would crush delicate leaves if tossed in a bowl.

Most supermarkets now carry a wide selection of salad mixes, all washed and ready to serve in transparent bags. One of the most popular is mesclun, an assortment of baby lettuces and other greens, such as radicchio and kale. In the South of France, mesclun is a salad mix that is very carefully blended with many different greens to give a delicate-tasting, colorful balance of sweet and bitter flavors, and often includes edible flowers. The problem with our commercially prepared mesclun is that it is usually blended for looks alone, and can be very bitter. Give mesclun a try, but if it is too bitter for your taste, balance the mix with a head of mild Boston or red leaf lettuce.

# Butter Lettuce with Apricot and Poppy Seed Dressing

MAKES 4 TO 6 SERVINGS

This sweet-and-sour dressing is good and thick, and works best spooned over tender butter (or Boston) lettuce leaves, not tossed.

**APRICOT AND POPPY SEED DRESSING**

¼ CUP APRICOT PRESERVES

3 TABLESPOONS CIDER VINEGAR

1 TEASPOON DRY MUSTARD

½ TEASPOON SALT

¼ TEASPOON FRESHLY GROUND BLACK PEPPER

½ CUP VEGETABLE OIL

1 TABLESPOON POPPY SEEDS

**FOR THE SALAD**

2 LARGE HEADS BUTTER OR BOSTON LETTUCE, RINSED AND DRIED

1 LARGE CARROT, GRATED (OPTIONAL)

**1.** To make the dressing, place the preserves, vinegar, mustard, salt, and pepper in a blender. With the machine running, gradually add the oil until thickened. Stir in the poppy seeds. (Don't blend the seeds into the dressing, or they may pulverize.) Pour the dressing into a sauceboat.

**2.** Arrange the lettuce leaves on individual salad plates. Serve, with the dressing passed on the side. If desired, sprinkle the dressed greens with the grated carrot.

# Green Salad with Green Ranchera Dressing

MAKES 4 SERVINGS

I love Green Goddess dressing, that pale green concoction that has been a favorite in San Francisco (and elsewhere) ever since it was named for a play that was passing through the City by the Bay in the early 1900s. No one remembers the play, but that dressing sure made an impression! My version stirs its essentials (anchovies and tarragon) into that Texas classic, ranch dressing, to make a delicious hybrid.

**GREEN RANCHERA DRESSING**

¼ CUP CHILLED BUTTERMILK

1 SCALLION, WHITE AND GREEN PARTS, COARSELY CHOPPED

3 TABLESPOONS CHOPPED FRESH PARSLEY

2 OIL-PACKED ANCHOVY FILLETS, RINSED, OR 1 TEASPOON ANCHOVY PASTE

1 TABLESPOON CHOPPED FRESH TARRAGON, OR 1 TEASPOON DRIED

1 GARLIC CLOVE, CRUSHED AND PEELED

¼ TEASPOON SALT

¼ TEASPOON FRESHLY GROUND BLACK PEPPER

¾ CUP MAYONNAISE

**FOR THE SALAD**

1 HEAD ROMAINE LETTUCE, TORN INTO BITE-SIZE PIECES, RINSED, AND DRIED

2 RIPE MEDIUM TOMATOES, SLICED

1 MEDIUM CUCUMBER, PEELED AND SLICED

1 SMALL ONION, CUT INTO THIN RINGS

**1.** To make the dressing, in a blender, puree all of the ingredients except the mayonnaise. Add the mayonnaise and pulse until mixed. Transfer to a small bowl.

**2.** In individual salad bowls, place the lettuce, tomato slices, cucumber, and onion rings. Serve the salad, with the dressing passed on the side.

# Iceberg Lettuce Wedges with Retro Roquefort Dressing

Here's one of those big, bold, thick-enough-for-a-spoon-to-stand-up-in blue cheese dressings. It's unbeatable when served on ice-cold iceberg lettuce wedges. Don't give me any grief for suggesting iceberg lettuce, as it is an honorable variety whose neutral flavor makes it indispensable with hearty dressings like this one. If you can find a farmstand that grows heirloom iceberg lettuce, you're really in for a treat.

**REAL ROQUEFORT DRESSING**

1 CUP MAYONNAISE

½ CUP SOUR CREAM

6 OUNCES ROQUEFORT CHEESE OR DANISH BLUE CHEESE, CRUMBLED

1 SCALLION, WHITE AND GREEN PARTS, MINCED

2 TABLESPOONS FRESH LEMON JUICE

1 GARLIC CLOVE, CRUSHED THROUGH A PRESS

½ TEASPOON COARSELY CRACKED BLACK PEPPERCORNS (CRUSHED IN A MORTAR OR UNDER A HEAVY SKILLET)

¼ TEASPOON SALT

**FOR THE SALAD**

1 LARGE HEAD ICEBERG LETTUCE, RINSED, DRIED, AND TORN INTO 4 OR 6 WEDGES

**1.** To make the dressing, combine all of the ingredients in a small bowl. Cover and refrigerate for at least 30 minutes to let the flavors blend.

**2.** Place the iceberg lettuce wedges on a baking sheet. Freeze the lettuce until very well chilled, about 10 minutes. Do not freeze the lettuce until it wilts—you just want it to chill thoroughly.

**3.** Place each lettuce wedge on a chilled plate, and spoon the dressing over each wedge. Serve immediately.

I couldn't cook without garlic, or at least I wouldn't want to. Most recipes call for chopped garlic, which is okay if the hard little garlic pieces will be softened by cooking. However, in other recipes, such as salad dressings or some salsas, the garlic will remain raw. In that case, I often puree the cloves so the garlic flavor will be better distributed and to keep my guests from biting into a piece of raw garlic (which can be an eye-opener, to say the least). Of course, the easiest way to puree garlic is in a garlic press. If you don't have a garlic press, you can make garlic paste by hand. Mince the garlic on a work surface, then sprinkle it with a bit of salt. Continue chopping the garlic, occasionally mashing and smearing it on the work surface with the side of the chopping knife, until it forms a paste. Scrape up the garlic paste with the knife. When seasoning the dish, remember that the garlic has some salt already, so use a lighter hand.

# Mixed Greens with Italian Thousand Island Dressing

Who says the "islands" in thousand island dressing have to be pickle relish? With sun-dried tomatoes, pimiento-stuffed olives, and capers, this old standard gets a Mediterranean makeover.

**ITALIAN THOUSAND ISLAND DRESSING**

¾ CUP MAYONNAISE

⅓ CUP DRAINED AND FINELY CHOPPED SUN-DRIED
  TOMATOES IN OIL

¼ CUP FINELY CHOPPED PIMIENTO-STUFFED GREEN
  OLIVES

2 TABLESPOONS BOTTLED CAPERS, RINSED,
  CHOPPED IF LARGE

2 TABLESPOONS AMERICAN-STYLE CHILI SAUCE OR CATSUP

¼ TEASPOON CRUSHED HOT RED PEPPER FLAKES

3 TABLESPOONS MILK, APPROXIMATELY

**FOR THE SALAD**

1 MEDIUM HEAD ROMAINE LETTUCE, TORN INTO BITE-SIZE
  PIECES

1 SMALL HEAD RADICCHIO, TORN INTO BITE-SIZE PIECES

**1.** To make the dressing, in a bowl, mix the mayonnaise, sun-dried tomatoes, olives, capers, chili sauce, and red pepper flakes. Stir in enough milk to thin to desired consistency. Cover and set aside at room temperature for 30 minutes to let the flavors blend, or cover and refrigerate for up to 2 days. (The dressing will thicken upon standing. Thin with milk or water as needed.)

**2.** Combine the lettuce and radicchio in a large bowl. Serve in salad bowls, with the dressing passed on the side.

# Korean Kim Chee Slaw

Korean restaurants are opening up all over the country—remember, it wasn't so long ago that Thai food was considered exotic. One of the most interesting parts of a Korean meal is the assortment of relishes served, which always include a very spicy pickled cabbage called *kim chee*. This slaw, great as a side salad for any Asian main course, borrows *kim chee*'s flavors, but tones them down a bit.

¼ CUP RICE VINEGAR

2 TABLESPOONS ASIAN DARK SESAME OIL

1 TABLESPOON FRESHLY SQUEEZED GINGER JUICE
   (SEE BELOW)

2 GARLIC CLOVES, CRUSHED THROUGH A PRESS

1 TEASPOON SUGAR

½ TEASPOON SALT

¼ TEASPOON CAYENNE PEPPER, OR MORE TO TASTE

½ CUP VEGETABLE OIL

4 CUPS SHREDDED NAPA CABBAGE
   (ABOUT ½ MEDIUM HEAD)

3 MEDIUM CARROTS, GRATED

2 SCALLIONS, WHITE AND GREEN PARTS, THINLY SLICED

**1.** In a small bowl, whisk together the vinegar, sesame oil, ginger juice, garlic, sugar, salt, and cayenne. Gradually whisk in the vegetable oil.

**2.** In a medium bowl, combine the cabbage, carrots, and scallions. Add the dressing and toss well. Serve immediately or cover and chill for up to 4 hours (the salad will wilt if held for longer than 4 hours, but it will still be good).

Ginger juice is a great secret ingredient, giving the spicy taste of ginger without the texture of the chopped root, which isn't appropriate for certain dishes. Choose a fresh ginger root with a smooth, tight skin—old, wrinkled ginger won't be as juicy. Just grate the ginger (it is unnecessary to peel) on the large holes of a cheese grater. You will need about 2 tablespoons of grated ginger to get 1 tablespoon of juice. Place the grated ginger in a clean kitchen towel. Over a small bowl, twist and wring the ginger in the towel to extract the juice.

# Roasted Beet and Vidalia Onion Salad

MAKES 6 TO 8 SERVINGS

Balsamic vinegar was made for this salad, a tantalizing mix of crisp and tender, red and white, and sweet and pungent. Many cooks have recently discovered the wonderful flavor of roasted beets, and people who hated canned beets are newfound beet fanatics. I like to roast beets on the gas grill, but I've also listed a number of options.

8 MEDIUM BEETS (ABOUT 1½ POUNDS BEETS), RINSED AND SCRUBBED

3 TABLESPOONS BALSAMIC VINEGAR

1 TABLESPOON FRESH TARRAGON, OR 1 TEASPOON DRIED

1 TEASPOON LIGHT BROWN SUGAR

½ TEASPOON SALT

¼ TEASPOON FRESHLY GROUND BLACK PEPPER

⅓ CUP EXTRA-VIRGIN OLIVE OIL

1 LARGE SWEET ONION, SUCH AS VIDALIA, THINLY SLICED

**1.** Preheat a gas grill on high heat. Turn one burner off, then reduce the other burner(s) to medium. Individually wrap each beet in aluminum foil. Place the beets over the off area and cover. Cook, turning the beets occasionally, until just tender, 45 minutes to 1 hour. Cool completely. Peel and slice the beets into ½-inch-thick rounds.

**2.** In a medium bowl, whisk the balsamic vinegar, tarragon, brown sugar, salt, and pepper until combined. Gradually whisk in the oil until the dressing thickens. Add the beets and onion and toss well. Cover and refrigerate until chilled, at least 1 hour. Serve chilled.

**To grill the beets on a charcoal grill:** Build a charcoal fire in the center of the grill and let the coals burn until covered with white ash and very hot. (You should be able to hold your hand directly over the coals for only 1 to 2 seconds.) Leave the fire heaped in the center of the grill—do not spread out. Place the foil-wrapped beets around the outside perimeter of the grill, not over the coals. Cover and cook, turning the beets occasionally, until just tender, 45 minutes to 1 hour. If the beets still aren't tender, place them, still wrapped in their foil, directly on the coals (which will have burned down to cooler embers). Cover and continue roasting until tender.

**To roast the beets in an oven:** Preheat the oven to 400°F. Place the foil-wrapped beets on a baking sheet. Roast, without turning, until just tender, 45 minutes to 1 hour.

**To microwave the beets:** Individually wrap each beet in microwave-safe plastic wrap. Place around the outside edge of a microwave carousel. Cook on medium-high (75 percent) heat until just tender, 15 to 20 minutes. Let the beets stand for 5 minutes before testing for doneness.

# Spicy Cabbage and Radish Slaw

MAKES 8 TO 12 SERVINGS

Certain dishes (like any kind of barbecued rib) just call out for slaw. This one has two secret ingredients to give it punch: grated radishes and a big spoonful of your favorite barbecue sauce.

¼ CUP BOTTLED OR HOMEMADE BARBECUE SAUCE

2 TABLESPOONS CIDER VINEGAR

1 TEASPOON CELERY SEEDS

1 TEASPOON SALT

¼ TEASPOON FRESHLY GROUND BLACK PEPPER

¾ CUP VEGETABLE OIL

8 CUPS SHREDDED GREEN CABBAGE (1 SMALL HEAD)

1½ CUPS GRATED RADISHES (ABOUT 8 LARGE RADISHES)

4 SCALLIONS, WHITE AND GREEN PARTS, MINCED

**1.** In a large bowl, whisk together the barbecue sauce, vinegar, celery seeds, salt, and pepper. Gradually whisk in the oil. Add the cabbage, radishes, and scallions and mix well.

**2.** Cover and refrigerate until chilled, at least 1 hour. Serve chilled.

# Grilled Zucchini Salad with Balsamic Sage Vinaigrette

MAKES 8 SERVINGS

Salads like this are served as antipasti in Italy's trattorias. Sage is a popular Tex-Mex flavor, but it doesn't work all that well raw, and needs to be heated to mellow it out. Making a quickly infused oil is the perfect way to solve the problem. You may use other fresh herbs, but for this dish, keep the dried ones in the kitchen cabinet.

6 MEDIUM ZUCCHINI, SCRUBBED (ABOUT 3 POUNDS)

½ CUP PLUS 2 TABLESPOONS EXTRA-VIRGIN OLIVE OIL

2 TABLESPOONS CHOPPED FRESH SAGE

2 TABLESPOONS BALSAMIC VINEGAR

¼ TEASPOON SALT

¼ TEASPOON FRESHLY GROUND BLACK PEPPER

**1.** Build a charcoal fire in an outdoor grill and let the coals burn until covered with white ash. (Or preheat a gas grill on high.) Lightly oil the grill grate.

**2.** Using a sharp knife, trim the stem ends of the zucchini. Slice each zucchini lengthwise into 3 or 4 strips about ¹/₂ inch wide. Place in a shallow baking dish and toss with 2 tablespoons of the olive oil. Grill the zucchini, turning once, until nicely browned with grill markings on both sides, 4 to 5 minutes. The zucchini should be tender, but still hold its shape. Transfer to a shallow nonmetal serving dish.

**3.** Meanwhile, in a small saucepan, heat the ¹/₂ cup oil and the sage over medium-low heat just until tiny bubbles appear around the sage, about 3 minutes. (Or place in a glass measuring cup and microwave on high for 45 to 60 seconds.) Let stand until completely cool.

**4.** In a small bowl, whisk the vinegar with the salt and pepper. Gradually whisk in the oil. Pour over the zucchini and let stand at room temperature until cool. Serve at room temperature.

**Variations**

Make the salad with half zucchini and half yellow summer squash.

You may not want to grill the zucchini. It can be broiled, of course, but sautéing in extra-virgin olive oil is a better option. Cook the zucchini in a large skillet over medium-high heat, turning once, until lightly browned on both sides, about 4 minutes. Do not salt the zucchini until after cooking, or it will not brown.

Olive oil is an indispensable ingredient in a good cook's kitchen. I use two different kinds of olive oil. Regular (formerly called pure) olive oil is golden yellow, and is best used for general cooking methods, like sautéing, where a mild olive flavor is appropriate. Extra-virgin olive oil, with its green tint, is much stronger tasting. While it can be used for cooking, it should be reserved for salad dressings and other dishes where its bold flavor can be appreciated.

# Horseradish Potato Salad

MAKES 4 SERVINGS

There are certain dishes that are meant to be served with steak—baked potatoes, onion rings, french fries. This tangy, creamy, chunky concoction belongs in this Steak Side Dish Hall of Fame. Add as much horseradish as you like.

2 POUNDS RED-SKINNED POTATOES (ABOUT 8 MEDIUM)

¾ CUP SOUR CREAM

⅓ CUP MAYONNAISE

2 TABLESPOONS PREPARED HORSERADISH,
    OR MORE TO TASTE

3 TABLESPOONS MINCED FRESH CHIVES, OR 1 SCALLION,
    WHITE AND GREEN PARTS, MINCED

½ TEASPOON SALT

¼ TEASPOON FRESHLY GROUND BLACK PEPPER

**1.** Place the potatoes in a medium saucepan and add enough cold water to cover. Bring to a boil over high heat. Add salt to taste, reduce the heat to medium-high, and cook until the potatoes are just tender when pierced with the tip of a sharp knife, 15 to 20 minutes. Drain well and rinse under cold water until easy to handle. If you wish, peel the potatoes, but I keep them unpeeled.

**2.** Meanwhile, in a medium bowl, mix the sour cream, mayonnaise, horseradish, chives, salt, and pep-per. Slice the potatoes into the bowl and mix. Serve immediately, or cover with plastic wrap and refrigerate until ready to serve.

To quick-chill cooked potatoes so you can enjoy a potato salad sooner, tilt the pan of potatoes to pour out the cooking water. Fill the pan with ice cubes. Place the pan under cold running water and fill it up. Let stand until the potatoes are cooled, about 5 minutes. Drain well.

# Black, Yellow, and Red Salad with Lime Vinaigrette

MAKES 8 SERVINGS

This is a big salad for summer dog days (or evenings) when you want something light for supper. It's great on its own, but keep it in mind to dress up simple grilled meats and poultry.

### LIME VINAIGRETTE

3 TABLESPOONS FRESH LIME JUICE

2 TEASPOONS GROUND MILD CHILE PEPPER, SUCH AS CHIMAYO

½ TEASPOON SALT

½ CUP EXTRA-VIRGIN OLIVE OIL

### FOR THE SALAD

4 CUPS COOKED BLACK BEANS, OR TWO 15-OUNCE CANS BLACK BEANS, DRAINED AND RINSED

2 CUPS CORN KERNELS, CUT FROM GRILLED CORN, OR 2 CUPS THAWED FROZEN CORN KERNELS

2 CUPS CHERRY TOMATOES, CUT INTO HALVES

4 SCALLIONS, WHITE AND GREEN PARTS, CHOPPED

⅓ CUP CHOPPED FRESH CILANTRO OR BASIL

1 CUP GRATED SHARP CHEDDAR CHEESE

**1.** To make the vinaigrette, whisk together the lime juice, chile pepper, and salt in a small bowl. Gradually whisk in the oil.

**2.** In a large bowl, combine the beans, corn, tomatoes, scallions, and cilantro. Add the dressing and mix well. Cover and refrigerate for at least 1 hour before serving. Just before serving, sprinkle with the cheese.

Nothing could be easier than grilling corn. Many cooks fret too much over this simple chore by peeling back the leaves, removing the silks, replacing the husk, tying them in place with string, and then soaking in water. Whew! Listen to me: Just throw the unhusked corn on a grill over hot coals (use high heat on a gas grill). That's it. Cook the corn, turning occasionally, until the silks are burned black and the husks are charred on all sides, 15 to 20 minutes. That charring adds a nice smoky flavor, too. Cool the corn slightly before removing the husks and silks—but you may want to protect your hands with a kitchen towel or gloves.

# Antipasti Pasta Salad with Giardinera, Salami, and Provolone

Pasta salad—just when you think you've seen them all, another comes along to remind you how good they can be. This colorful addition to the roster is the one to make when you need a pasta salad that is loaded with flavor but takes very little effort.

**ITALIAN VINAIGRETTE**

⅓ CUP RED WINE VINEGAR

2 GARLIC CLOVES, CRUSHED THROUGH A PRESS

½ TEASPOON DRIED OREGANO

½ TEASPOON SALT

¼ TEASPOON CRUSHED HOT RED PEPPER FLAKES

⅔ CUP OLIVE OIL

**TO COMPLETE THE RECIPE**

1 POUND BOW-TIE PASTA

ONE 24-OUNCE JAR ITALIAN-STYLE MARINATED VEGETABLES (*GIARDINERA*), DRAINED AND COARSELY CHOPPED

ONE 7-OUNCE JAR ROASTED RED PEPPERS, DRAINED AND CHOPPED

8 OUNCES SHARP PROVOLONE CHEESE, CUT INTO ½-INCH CUBES

4 OUNCES THINLY SLICED SALAMI, CUT INTO ¼-INCH-THICK STRIPS

2 CELERY RIBS, FINELY CHOPPED

½ CUP PITTED, COARSELY CHOPPED BLACK OR GREEN MEDITERRANEAN OLIVES

2 TABLESPOONS CHOPPED FRESH PARSLEY

**1.** To make the vinaigrette, whisk together the vinegar, garlic, oregano, salt, and red pepper flakes in a medium bowl. Gradually whisk in the oil. Set aside.

**2.** Bring a large pot of lightly salted water to a boil over high heat. Add the pasta and cook until tender, about 9 minutes. Drain, rinse under cold running water, and drain well. Transfer to a large bowl.

**3.** Add the *giardinera*, roasted red peppers, provolone, salami, celery, olives, and parsley. Toss to combine, and mix in the reserved dressing. Cover and refrigerate until chilled, at least 1 hour or up to overnight. Serve chilled or at room temperature.

# Orange and Pomegranate Salad

Is it a salad, or is it a salsa? This chunky, refreshing mixture is the perfect accompaniment to the Roast Pork Tenderloin with Pomegranate Sauce on page 96. Pomegranates have crunchy tiny seeds. Tell your fellow diners that it's okay to eat them.

1 TABLESPOON RED WINE VINEGAR

1 TABLESPOON LIGHT BROWN SUGAR

⅛ TEASPOON SALT

1 TABLESPOON EXTRA-VIRGIN OLIVE OIL

3 NAVEL ORANGES, SECTIONED, COARSELY CHOPPED

½ CUP POMEGRANATE SEEDS (SEE PAGE 96)

½ CUP PITTED AND CHOPPED BLACK MEDITERRANEAN OLIVES

1 JALAPEÑO PEPPER, SEEDED AND MINCED

1½ TEASPOONS CHOPPED FRESH ROSEMARY, OR ½ TEASPOON DRIED

**1.** In a medium bowl, whisk together the vinegar, brown sugar, and salt, then add the oil. Add the oranges, pomegranate seeds, olives, jalapeño, and rosemary and mix.

**2.** Cover and refrigerate until ready to serve, but no longer than 1 hour, or the flavors will get muddled.

# Mexican Fire and Ice
# Fruit Salad

## MAKES 6 TO 8 SERVINGS

Just as many American families serve a creamy fruit salad at holiday buffets, the Mexican menu includes *ensalada de Noche Buena,* or Christmas Eve salad, a marvelous combination of colors, textures, and flavors with the surprising punch of chile pepper. The idea of fruit salad with peppers may strike some unadventuresome eaters as odd, but don't knock it 'til you've tried it, especially with grilled pork or swordfish or roast ham.

Resist the temptation to mix the salad and dressing together hours ahead and chill until serving. The fruit will release too much juice and dilute the dressing, and the chile pepper will overpower the salad. You want a juxtaposition of flavors, not a mishmash.

2 MEDIUM APPLES, SUCH AS GRANNY SMITH, PEELED, CORED, AND CUT INTO ½-INCH CUBES

½ RIPE MEDIUM PINEAPPLE, PARED, CORED, AND CUT INTO ½-INCH CUBES (ABOUT 2 CUPS)

2 NAVEL ORANGES, PEELED AND CUT INTO SEGMENTS

1 TABLESPOON FRESH LIME JUICE

2 TABLESPOONS MAYONNAISE

2 TABLESPOONS SOUR CREAM

1 TABLESPOON CHOPPED FRESH MINT

1 JALAPEÑO PEPPER, SEEDED AND MINCED

GRATED ZEST OF 1 LIME

1 TABLESPOON GROUND MILD CHILE PEPPER, SUCH AS CHIMAYO (OPTIONAL)

⅓ CUP POMEGRANATE SEEDS (SEE PAGE 96)

⅓ CUP CHOPPED UNSALTED PEANUTS

**1.** In a large bowl, combine the apples, pineapple, oranges, and lime juice. Cover and refrigerate until well chilled, at least 2 hours. (If the fruit was chilled before preparation, you can proceed.)

**2.** When ready to serve, drain any collected juices from the fruit. In a medium bowl, mix the mayonnaise, sour cream, mint, jalapeño, and lime zest. Pour over the

fruit and toss gently. Taste for seasoning, and if you think it could use a little more heat, add the ground chile pepper. Sprinkle with the pomegranate seeds and peanuts. Serve chilled.

To segment oranges and other citrus fruit, use a serrated knife to cut thin slices off the top and bottom of the fruit. Stand the fruit on one end to stabilize it. Cut off the skin in large pieces where the white pith meets the fruit. Hold the peeled fruit over a bowl. To release the fruit segments, cut between the interior membranes of the fruit, reaching down to the core, and let the segments fall into the bowl as they are cut. This is a very useful technique to know, but otherwise, simply slice the orange into $1/3$-inch-thick rounds. If your fruit has seeds, pick them out with the tip of a sharp knife.

# main-course soups

SOUP FOR SUPPER. DOESN'T THAT HAVE A NICE RING TO IT? I'M NOT TALKING ABOUT THE kind of delicate, appetite-teasing soup you'd serve as a first course, but a hearty, rib-sticking pot of soup that a spoon would practically stand up in. The kind of soup you eat with a fork and a knife, as well as a spoon. In other words, a soup that is so satisfying that it's a whole meal, accompanied by a chunk of bread.

Soup is only as good as its ingredients, especially its stock. Food writers like to talk about the benefits of having a stash of homemade stock in the freezer. These days my son's Popsicles have taken over the spot where the stock once was. If you have the time to make your own stock, then please go ahead and do it. But as all of the soups in this chapter get plenty of flavor from meat and vegetables, I am happy to use a good canned broth. Low-sodium canned broth has the best flavor. Many supermarkets, specialty stores, and butchers are now carrying their own freshly made stocks, refrigerated or frozen. Just don't resort to a bouillon cube, and your soup will be fine.

The same argument can be made about freshly cooked beans versus canned beans. If you are a from-scratch cook, you'll cook your own beans. But when beans are being used in a soup as just one ingredient in many, I use canned ones without a twinge of guilt. (The exception is the White Bean and Garlic Soup with Grilled Sausage, which should be prepared with dried beans.) As with canned broth, search out a good brand and remain loyal to it. Canned beans should be firm and tasty, and not too salty.

Two other convenience foods, frozen peas and frozen corn, find their way into some of my dishes, because the frozen versions are often more reliably flavorful than the fresh. To quickly defrost them, place the frozen vegetables in a wire sieve and rinse under cold running water until thawed, about 3 minutes. Of course, you can also defrost them in a microwave oven, but the rinsing method keeps them from overcooking.

# Caribbean Beef, Acorn Squash, and Kale Soup

Unless you live in the Caribbean, this combination of ingredients will seem unfamiliar, but trust me and try it. Even more than other soups, every ingredient seems to contribute a little something special, adding up to a big bowl of flavor. Pickapeppa sauce is a Caribbean condiment that has a sweet and spicy flavor. It can be found in the hot sauce department of many supermarkets and specialty stores.

3 TABLESPOONS VEGETABLE OIL

1 POUND BEEF CHUCK, CUT INTO 1-INCH CUBES

1 MEDIUM ONION, CHOPPED

1 MEDIUM CARROT, CHOPPED

1 MEDIUM CELERY STALK, CHOPPED

2 GARLIC CLOVES, MINCED

3½ CUPS BEEF BROTH, PREFERABLY HOMEMADE,
    OR USE LOW-SODIUM CANNED BROTH

½ CUP DRY SHERRY

1 TEASPOON DRIED THYME

1 BAY LEAF

½ TEASPOON SALT

½ TEASPOON FRESHLY GROUND BLACK PEPPER

ONE 1½-POUND ACORN SQUASH, HALVED, SEEDS REMOVED,
    CUT INTO 1-INCH CUBES, AND PARED (SEE NOTE)

12 OUNCES KALE, TOUGH STEMS REMOVED, AND LEAVES
    CUT INTO THIN SHREDS

PICKAPEPPA SAUCE, FOR SERVING (OPTIONAL)

**1.** In a Dutch oven or flameproof casserole, heat 2 tablespoons oil over medium-high heat. In batches, add the beef and brown on all sides, about 8 minutes. Transfer to a plate and set aside.

**2.** Add the remaining 1 tablespoon oil to the Dutch oven and reduce the heat to medium. Add the onion, carrot, celery, and garlic. Cook, stirring occasionally, until the vegetables soften, about 5 minutes. Return the beef to the pot. Add the broth and sherry and 2 cups cold water. Bring to a boil over high heat, skimming off any foam that rises to the surface. Add the thyme, bay leaf, salt, and pepper. Reduce the heat to medium-low and partially cover. Simmer for 1 hour.

**3.** Stir in the squash and kale. Cook until the meat is tender, about 30 more minutes. Serve in deep soup bowls, with the optional Pickapeppa sauce passed on the side for seasoning.

The easiest way to pare acorn squash is to cut the squash into cubes, then pare away the skin from each cube. You're asking for trouble if you try to pare a large chunk.

# Border Chicken and Fideo Noodle Soup

### MAKES 6 SERVINGS

Chicken thighs make great soup—they hold up to long simmering better than breasts, and have a good, meaty texture, too. Thin, Mexican-style *fideo* noodles, twisted into skeins, give this chicken noodle soup its border sensibility. If necessary, substitute angel hair pasta, broken into 2-inch pieces.

2 TABLESPOONS OLIVE OIL

6 CHICKEN THIGHS (2¼ POUNDS)

6 OUNCES *FIDEOS* (THIN EGG NOODLES IN SKEINS)

ONE 35-OUNCE CAN TOMATOES IN JUICE, DRAINED

1 MEDIUM ONION, COARSELY CHOPPED

1 MEDIUM GREEN PEPPER, SEEDED AND COARSELY
   CHOPPED

1 JALAPEÑO PEPPER, SEEDED AND COARSELY CHOPPED

2 GARLIC CLOVES, CRUSHED UNDER A KNIFE

2 CUPS CHICKEN BROTH, PREFERABLY HOMEMADE,
   OR USE LOW-SODIUM CANNED BROTH

1 TEASPOON DRIED OREGANO

½ TEASPOON GROUND CUMIN

¼ TEASPOON CRUMBLED SAFFRON THREADS (OPTIONAL)

½ TEASPOON SALT

¼ TEASPOON FRESHLY GROUND BLACK PEPPER

1 CUP FRESH OR THAWED FROZEN CORN KERNELS

**1.** In a Dutch oven or soup pot, heat 1 tablespoon of the oil over medium-high heat. Rinse the chicken and pat dry with paper towels. Add the chicken thighs to the pot, skin side down, and cook, turning occasionally, until browned, about 6 minutes. Transfer the chicken to a plate, leaving the fat in the Dutch oven, and set aside.

**2.** Add the *fideos* and cook, turning once, until browned on both sides, about 2 minutes. Transfer to a

plate and set aside. Pour out any fat remaining in the pot, and wipe the pot clean with paper towels.

**3.** Add the remaining 1 tablespoon oil to the pot and heat. In a food processor or blender, puree the tomatoes, onion, green pepper, jalapeño, and garlic. Pour into the pot and bring to a boil. Return the chicken to the pot. Add the broth and 3 cups water. Bring to a simmer, skimming off any foam that rises to the surface. Add the oregano, cumin, optional saffron, and salt and pepper. Reduce the heat to medium-low and cover partially. Simmer until the chicken is tender, about 45 minutes.

**4.** Remove the chicken from the pot. Discard the skin and bones, and cut the chicken into bite-size pieces. Return the chicken to the pot, along with the *fideos* and corn. Increase the heat to medium and cook at a brisk simmer until the *fideos* are tender, about 10 minutes. Serve in individual soup bowls.

# My Tortilla Soup

This recipe appeared in my *Tortillas* cookbook, but as it is one of my favorite supper soups, I am including it in this collection, too. Chunky with chicken, tomatoes, and chickpeas, it would be easier to eat with a fork than a spoon, but I'll let you make that decision. I used to deep-fry the tortillas, but now they are crisped in the oven.

NINE 6-INCH CORN TORTILLAS, CUT INTO ¼-INCH-WIDE
    STRIPS
NONSTICK VEGETABLE OIL SPRAY
2 TABLESPOONS OLIVE OIL
ONE 3½-POUND CHICKEN, CUT INTO 8 PIECES
2 MEDIUM ONIONS, CHOPPED
3 MEDIUM CARROTS, CUT INTO ¼-INCH ROUNDS
8 GARLIC CLOVES, MINCED
¾ TEASPOON DRIED OREGANO
¾ TEASPOON DRIED MARJORAM
2 BAY LEAVES

4 CUPS CHICKEN BROTH, PREFERABLY HOMEMADE, OR
    USE LOW-SODIUM CANNED BROTH
¾ CUP CHOPPED CANNED TOMATOES
2 TABLESPOONS CHOPPED CANNED MILD GREEN CHILES
3 *CHIPOTLES EN ADOBO*, CHOPPED, WITH THEIR SAUCE
2 CUPS COOKED AND DRAINED CHICKPEAS, OR
    USE ONE 19-OUNCE CAN, DRAINED AND RINSED
1⅓ CUPS THAWED FROZEN GREEN PEAS
2 PACKED CUPS COARSELY CHOPPED FRESH SPINACH LEAVES
SALT

**1.** Position the racks in the center and top third of the oven and preheat to 350°F. Spread the tortilla strips on baking sheets and spray with the nonstick spray. Bake, stirring occasionally, until toasted, 12 to 15 minutes. Set aside.

**2.** In a Dutch oven or flameproof casserole, heat the oil over medium heat. Rinse the chicken and pat dry with paper towels. In batches, add the chicken, skin side down, and cook, turning occasionally, until browned, about 10 minutes. Transfer to a plate. Pour off all but 2 tablespoons fat from the pot. Add the onions, carrots, garlic, oregano, marjoram, and bay leaves to the pot. Cover and cook, stirring occasionally and scraping the bottom of the pan, for 10 minutes.

**3.** Return the chicken to the pot. Add the broth, 4 cups water, the tomatoes, green chiles, and chipotles and bring to a simmer. Reduce the heat to medium-low and cover partially. Simmer until the chicken is tender, about 30 minutes. Discard the skin and bones, and shred the chicken meat. Return the chicken to the pot.

**4.** Add the chickpeas and peas, return to a simmer, and cook until heated through, about 5 minutes. Stir in the spinach. Season with the salt. Serve in individual soup bowls, topping each serving with a generous handful of tortilla strips.

# Fork and Knife Chicken Soup with Chile-Corn Dumplings

## MAKES 4 TO 6 SERVINGS

Chicken and dumplings are about as "supper" as you can get. No need to make this soup with chicken broth—you will get plenty of flavor from just a big chicken and water.

ONE 4-POUND CHICKEN

1 TABLESPOON VEGETABLE OIL

1 MEDIUM ONION, CHOPPED

2 MEDIUM CARROTS, CHOPPED

2 MEDIUM CELERY RIBS WITH LEAVES, CHOPPED

2 TABLESPOONS CHOPPED FRESH PARSLEY

1 TEASPOON DRIED THYME

½ TEASPOON DRIED SAGE

½ TEASPOON SALT

¼ TEASPOON FRESHLY GROUND BLACK PEPPER

FOR THE DUMPLINGS

1 CUP ALL-PURPOSE FLOUR

2 TEASPOONS BAKING POWDER

1½ TEASPOONS CHILI POWDER

½ TEASPOON SALT

1 LARGE EGG

¼ CUP PLUS 2 TABLESPOONS MILK

½ CUP FRESH OR THAWED FROZEN CORN KERNELS

**1.** Using a large knife, cut the leg portions from the chicken. Cut at the knee joint to make 2 drumsticks and 2 thighs. Cut the back off the chicken. Cut the breast in half lengthwise to make 2 halves. Cut the wing from each breast, leaving about one-third of the breast attached to the wings (this makes the skimpy wings into larger servings). Rinse the chicken and pat dry with paper towels.

**2.** In a Dutch oven or flameproof casserole, heat the oil over medium-high heat. In batches without crowding, brown the chicken parts on all sides, about

10 minutes. Transfer the chicken to a plate and set aside.

**3.** Pour off all but 2 tablespoons fat from the pot. Add the onion, carrots, and celery. Cook, stirring occasionally, until the vegetables soften, about 5 minutes. Return the chicken to the pot and add enough cold water to cover by 1 inch (about 5½ cups). Bring to a boil over high heat, skimming off the foam that rises to the surface. Stir in the parsley, thyme, and sage. Reduce the heat to medium-low and cover. Simmer until the chicken is almost tender, about 35 minutes. Remove and discard the chicken back. Season the soup with the salt and pepper.

**4.** To make the dumplings, sift the flour, baking powder, chili powder, and salt into a medium bowl. In a small bowl, whisk together the egg and milk. Stir into the dry ingredients to make a soft dough. Stir in the corn. Drop the dough by tablespoons onto the sim-

mering cooking liquid. Cover and cook until the dumplings are cooked through and the chicken is tender, 10 to 15 minutes.

**5.** For each serving, place a piece of chicken in a deep soup bowl. Ladle in the soup and top with a couple of dumplings. Serve immediately.

# Mexican Meatball Soup

Most Americans think that meatballs belong in spaghetti sauce, but south of the border, meatballs are most often found in soup. A sprinkle of fresh mint lightens the meaty broth.

**FOR THE MEATBALLS**

8 OUNCES GROUND BEEF

8 OUNCES GROUND PORK

⅓ CUP DRIED UNFLAVORED BREAD CRUMBS

1 LARGE EGG, BEATEN

2 TABLESPOONS CHOPPED FRESH PARSLEY

2 TEASPOONS CHILI POWDER

1 TEASPOON SALT

¼ TEASPOON DRIED OREGANO

¼ TEASPOON FRESHLY GROUND BLACK PEPPER

**FOR THE SOUP**

2 TABLESPOONS OLIVE OIL, PLUS MORE AS NEEDED

1 MEDIUM ONION, CHOPPED

2 MEDIUM CARROTS, CUT INTO ½-INCH CUBES

1 LARGE ZUCCHINI, CUT INTO ½-INCH CUBES

1 JALAPEÑO PEPPER, SEEDED AND MINCED

2 GARLIC CLOVES, MINCED

2 CUPS BEEF BROTH, PREFERABLY HOMEMADE, OR
   USE LOW-SODIUM CANNED BROTH

2 TABLESPOONS CHOPPED FRESH MINT, OR
   1½ TEASPOONS DRIED

¼ TEASPOON SALT

**1.** To make the meatballs, combine all of the ingredients in a medium bowl. Using a scant tablespoon for each, form into meatballs.

**2.** To make the soup, heat the oil in a Dutch oven or flameproof casserole over medium-high heat. In batches, add the meatballs and cook, turning occasionally, until browned, about 7 minutes. Using a slotted spoon, transfer the browned meatballs to paper towels and set aside.

**3.** Add the onion, carrots, zucchini, jalapeño, and garlic to the Dutch oven, adding more oil if needed.

Cook, stirring occasionally, until softened, about 5 minutes. Add 3 cups cold water and the broth and bring to a boil. Reduce the heat to medium-low and partially cover. Simmer for 30 minutes.

**4.** Add the meatballs to the soup and simmer until the vegetables are very tender and the meatballs are cooked through, about 15 minutes. Add the mint and season with the salt. Serve immediately in deep soup bowls.

# Sparerib and Hominy Soup

Pozole is a soupy pork and hominy stew with lots of friends on both sides of the border. This simplified version uses spareribs, which are a great soup ingredient—the bones give the broth extra body and flavor. The toppings allow guests to personalize their servings, so serve as many garnishes as you can manage.

2 TABLESPOONS OLIVE OIL, PLUS MORE AS NEEDED

2 POUNDS PORK SPARERIBS (HAVE THE BUTCHER
    CUT THEM BETWEEN THE BONES, THEN INTO
    1½-INCH LENGTHS)

1 LARGE ONION, CHOPPED

1 LARGE ZUCCHINI, CUT INTO ½-INCH CUBES

1 MEDIUM CUBANELLE OR GREEN BELL PEPPER,
    SEEDED AND CHOPPED

1 JALAPEÑO PEPPER, SEEDED AND MINCED

2 GARLIC CLOVES, MINCED

½ TEASPOON SALT

¼ TEASPOON FRESHLY GROUND BLACK PEPPER

4 CUPS CHICKEN BROTH, PREFERABLY HOMEMADE,
    OR USE LOW-SODIUM CANNED BROTH

2 TABLESPOONS CHOPPED FRESH CILANTRO OR PARSLEY

1 TABLESPOON DRIED OREGANO

ONE 15-OUNCE CAN HOMINY, RINSED AND DRAINED

*GARNISH:* GRATED RADISHES, CUBED AVOCADO, SLICED
    BLACK OLIVES, LIME WEDGES, GRATED MONTEREY JACK
    CHEESE, CHOPPED PICKLED JALAPEÑO PEPPERS

**1.** In a Dutch oven or soup pot, heat the oil over medium-high heat. In batches without crowding, add the spareribs and cook until browned on both sides, about 8 minutes. Transfer to a plate and set aside.

**2.** Adding more oil to the pot, if needed, add the onion, zucchini, Cubanelle and jalapeño peppers, and garlic. Cook, stirring often, until softened, about 5 minutes. Return the spareribs to the pot and season with the salt and pepper. Add the broth and bring to a boil over high heat, skimming off any foam that rises to the surface. Add the cilantro and oregano and reduce the heat to low. Cook, partially covered, until the spareribs are tender, about 1½ hours. During the last 5 minutes, stir in the hominy.

**3.** Place the garnishes in individual bowls for serving. Serve the soup in deep soup bowls, allowing each guest to add the garnishes to taste (and to use their fingers to eat the spareribs).

When most cooks want a mild green pepper, they use green bell peppers. Another delicious cooking pepper (as opposed to a seasoning hot chile pepper) is the Cubanelle. Also known as an Italian frying pepper, it is long and light green, with a somewhat more complex flavor than the familiar bell pepper.

# Double-Cooked Minestrone

MAKES 6 TO 8 SERVINGS

In an Italian kitchen, nothing goes to waste. Take yesterday's minestrone—it's layered with bread, sprinkled with cheese, and baked to make a kind of soup-casserole called *ribollita* (which literally means reboiled). The result is so delicious that I make the minestrone part just so it can be double-cooked.

¼ CUP EXTRA-VIRGIN OLIVE OIL, PLUS MORE FOR
    SERVING

1 LARGE ONION, CHOPPED

1 MEDIUM CARROT, CUT INTO ½-INCH CUBES

2 MEDIUM CELERY RIBS WITH LEAVES, CUT INTO
    ¼-INCH-THICK SLICES

1 LARGE ZUCCHINI, CUT INTO ½-INCH CUBES

2 GARLIC CLOVES, MINCED

4 CUPS CHOPPED GREEN CABBAGE
    (ABOUT ½ MEDIUM HEAD)

ONE 28-OUNCE CAN TOMATOES IN JUICE,
    DRAINED AND CHOPPED

2 TABLESPOONS CHOPPED FRESH PARSLEY

1 TEASPOON DRIED BASIL

1 TEASPOON DRIED OREGANO

¼ TEASPOON CRUSHED HOT RED PEPPER FLAKES

2 CUPS BEEF BROTH, PREFERABLY HOMEMADE, OR
    USE LOW-SODIUM CANNED BROTH

2 CUPS COOKED WHITE BEANS (CANNELLINI), OR
    ONE 19-OUNCE CAN, DRAINED AND RINSED

SALT

ABOUT 8 LARGE SLICES CRUSTY ITALIAN OR FRENCH BREAD,
    TOASTED

½ CUP FRESHLY GRATED PARMESAN CHEESE

**1.** In a Dutch oven or flameproof casserole, heat 2 tablespoons of the oil over medium heat. Add the onion, carrot, celery, zucchini, and garlic. Cook uncovered, stirring occasionally, until softened, about 5 minutes. Add the cabbage, cover, and cook until wilted, about 5 minutes. Stir in the tomatoes, parsley, basil, oregano, and red pepper flakes.

**2.** Add 3 cups cold water and the broth and bring to a boil. Reduce the heat to medium-low and partially cover. Simmer for 30 minutes. During the last 10 minutes, stir in the beans. Season with salt to taste.

**3.** Preheat the oven to 400°F. Arrange the bread on baking sheets and lightly brush with the remaining oil. Bake until the bread is lightly toasted around the edges, about 10 minutes. Set the toasted bread aside. Reduce the oven temperature to 350°F.

**4.** Add 4 bread slices to the soup, pressing into the soup until completely submerged. Place the remaining bread on the top of the soup and sprinkle with the cheese. Bake until the cheese is golden brown, about 20 minutes. Serve in deep soup bowls, including a piece of the crusty bread topping, and a cruet of additional olive oil for drizzling.

The exact amount of bread needed for a *ribollita* depends on the size of the loaf—you need a few slices to tuck into the soup to thicken it, plus enough to cover the top of the soup. Large round loaves work best. If you have to use a long loaf, slice the bread on a diagonal to make longer slices.

Use a high-quality, full-flavored extra-virgin olive oil for *ribollita*. The olive oil really seasons the dish, and is more than just a cooking medium for sautéing the vegetables.

# Curried Split Pea and
# Kielbasa Soup

MAKES 6 TO 8 SERVINGS

A dash of curry powder gives mellow split pea a nice jolt of spice. If you can find them (at Indian markets and some supermarkets), use yellow split peas, which cook into a deep gold puree to complement the color of the curry. Whenever I have a ham bone, I add it to the soup instead of the sausage, but the kielbasa adds a good hamlike flavor without having to make a ham first.

2 TABLESPOONS VEGETABLE OIL

1 POUND PORK OR TURKEY KIELBASA, CUT INTO
    ½-INCH-THICK ROUNDS

1 LARGE ONION, CHOPPED

2 MEDIUM CARROTS, CUT INTO ½-INCH PIECES

2 MEDIUM CELERY RIBS WITH LEAVES, CUT INTO
    ¼-INCH-THICK SLICES

2 TEASPOONS MADRAS-STYLE CURRY POWDER

1 POUND YELLOW OR GREEN SPLIT PEAS

2 MEDIUM RED-SKINNED POTATOES, SCRUBBED,
    CUT INTO ¾-INCH CUBES

2 CUP CHICKEN BROTH, PREFERABLY HOMEMADE, OR
    USE LOW-SODIUM CANNED BROTH

1 BAY LEAF

SALT

**1.** In a Dutch oven or flameproof casserole, heat the oil over medium-high heat. Add the kielbasa and cook until lightly browned, about 5 minutes. Using a slotted spoon, transfer to a plate and set aside.

**2.** Add the onion, carrots, and celery to the Dutch oven and cook, stirring occasionally, until softened, about 5 minutes. Add the curry and stir until fragrant, about 30 seconds. Add the split peas and potatoes. Stir in 4 cups cold water, the broth, and the bay leaf. Return the kielbasa to the Dutch oven. Bring to a boil over medium heat. Reduce the heat to low and partially cover. Simmer until the peas are very tender, about 1 hour.

**3.** Discard the bay leaf. Using a large spoon, crush the peas and potatoes into the soup until it is as thick as you like. Season with the salt. Serve in deep soup bowls.

### Variations

**Curried Split Pea Soup with Ham:** Delete the kielbasa. Add a meaty ham bone to the soup at the same time as the broth and cook for 1 hour. Remove the ham bone, cut off and cube any ham meat, and stir the ham meat back into the soup.

**Split Pea Soup with Dill:** Delete the curry powder. Stir 2 tablespoons chopped fresh dill into the soup during the last 10 minutes of cooking.

# Green Vegetable Soup with Cheese Gnocchi

Tender, plump puffs of Parmesan and ricotta cheeses float in a soup packed with a passel of green vegetables. This soup is light, but very satisfying, perfect for late summer meals.

**FOR THE SOUP**

2 TABLESPOONS OLIVE OIL

1 MEDIUM ONION, CHOPPED

8 OUNCES GREEN BEANS, CUT INTO ¾-INCH-LONG PIECES

1 MEDIUM ZUCCHINI, CUT INTO ½-INCH CUBES

1 MEDIUM CELERY RIB WITH LEAVES, CHOPPED

2 GARLIC CLOVES, MINCED

5 CUPS CHICKEN BROTH, PREFERABLY HOMEMADE, OR USE LOW-SODIUM CANNED BROTH

1 CUP FRESH OR THAWED FROZEN PEAS

1 TABLESPOON CHOPPED FRESH BASIL

½ TEASPOON SALT

¼ TEASPOON CRUSHED HOT RED PEPPER FLAKES

**FOR THE GNOCCHI**

1 CUP FRESHLY GRATED PARMESAN CHEESE

½ CUP RICOTTA CHEESE

¼ CUP ALL-PURPOSE FLOUR

1 LARGE EGG, BEATEN

1 TABLESPOON CHOPPED FRESH BASIL

¼ TEASPOON SALT

¼ TEASPOON FRESHLY GROUND BLACK PEPPER

**1.** In a Dutch oven or flameproof casserole, heat the oil over medium heat. Add the onion, green beans, zucchini, celery, and garlic. Cook, stirring occasionally, until the onion softens, about 5 minutes. Add the chicken broth and bring to a boil. Reduce the heat to medium-low and simmer until the vegetables are tender, about 30 minutes. During the last 10 minutes, add the peas (if using thawed peas, add during the last 5 minutes). Stir in the basil and season with the salt and red pepper flakes.

**2.** To make the gnocchi, mix all of the ingredients in a medium bowl until combined. Drop by scant tablespoons into the simmering soup. Partially cover the soup and simmer the gnocchi until cooked through, about 10 minutes. Serve in deep soup bowls.

# White Bean and Garlic Soup with Grilled Sausage

Long cooking tames the rip-roaring strength of garlic, so don't be alarmed at the twelve cloves that are simmered into this soup. The ham hock is important to flavor the beans, but after the beans are cooked, you may not want to add its meat to the soup, as you will be getting plenty of meat from the grilled sausage. While a sweet Italian sausage is most appropriate, experiment with other favorites—the soup is very versatile.

1 POUND DRIED WHITE BEANS, PREFERABLY CANNELLINI, RINSED AND SORTED

2 TABLESPOONS EXTRA-VIRGIN OLIVE OIL

1 LARGE ONION, CHOPPED

2 MEDIUM CARROTS, CUT INTO ½-INCH CUBES

2 MEDIUM CELERY RIBS WITH LEAVES, CUT INTO ¼-INCH-THICK SLICES

12 GARLIC CLOVES, CRUSHED UNDER A KNIFE AND PEELED

3½ CUPS CHICKEN BROTH, PREFERABLY HOMEMADE, OR USE LOW-SODIUM CANNED BROTH

ONE 12-OUNCE HAM HOCK

2 TEASPOONS CHOPPED FRESH SAGE, OR 1 TEASPOON DRIED

1 BAY LEAF

½ TEASPOON FRESHLY GROUND BLACK PEPPER

½ TEASPOON SALT

1 POUND PORK OR TURKEY SWEET ITALIAN SAUSAGE

**1.** Place the beans in a large bowl and add enough cold water to cover. Let stand for at least 4 hours or overnight. (Or place the beans in a large pot and add enough cold water to cover. Bring to a boil over high heat. Cook for 2 minutes. Remove from the heat, cover tightly, and let stand for 1 hour.) Drain.

**2.** In a large Dutch oven or flameproof casserole, heat the oil over medium heat. Add the onion, carrots, celery, and garlic. Cover and cook until the vegetables soften, about 5 minutes.

**3.** Add the beans, broth, 2½ cups cold water, the ham hock, sage, bay leaf, and pepper. Bring to a boil over high heat. Reduce the heat to low and partially cover. Cook until the beans are tender, about 1¼ hours. During the last 15 minutes, season with the salt. Discard the bay leaf. Remove the ham hock. In batches, puree the soup in a blender or food processor, and return to the pot. (If desired, discard the skin and bones from the ham hock, chop the meat, and stir the meat into the pureed soup.)

4. Meanwhile, build a charcoal fire in an outdoor grill or preheat a gas grill on high. Prick each sausage a few times with a fork. Place in a large saucepan and cover with cold water. Bring to a boil over medium heat. Cook for 2 minutes. Drain.

5. Grill the sausages, turning occasionally, until browned on all sides, about 10 minutes. Transfer to a cutting board and slice into $1/2$-inch-thick rounds. Stir the sausage into the soup. Serve in deep soup bowls.

# Southwestern Clam Chowder with Tequila Splash

MAKES 4 TO 6 SERVINGS

This chile-kissed chowder (a close relative to Manhattan chowder) gets even more interesting when seasoned with a splash of tequila. I make a "virgin" version, then allow the grownups to add the tequila to their bowl to taste.

1 TABLESPOON OLIVE OIL

3 OUNCES SMOKED CHORIZO LINKS, CHOPPED

1 MEDIUM ONION, CHOPPED

2 MEDIUM CELERY RIBS WITH LEAVES, CHOPPED

1 MEDIUM CUBANELLE OR SMALL GREEN BELL PEPPER, SEEDED AND CHOPPED

1 JALAPEÑO PEPPER, SEEDED AND MINCED

2 GARLIC CLOVES, MINCED

ONE 35-OUNCE CAN TOMATOES IN JUICE, DRAINED, JUICES RESERVED, AND CHOPPED

2 CUPS BOTTLED CLAM JUICE

1 TEASPOON DRIED MARJORAM

¼ TEASPOON CRUSHED HOT RED PEPPER FLAKES

24 LITTLENECK CLAMS, SCRUBBED AND SOAKED

TEQUILA, FOR SERVING (OPTIONAL)

**1.** In a Dutch oven or soup pot, heat the oil over medium heat. Add the chorizo and cook, stirring occasionally, until lightly browned, about 5 minutes. Add the onion, celery, Cubanelle and jalapeño peppers, and garlic. Cook until the onion softens, about 5 minutes.

**2.** Add the tomatoes with their juices, the clam juice, marjoram, and red pepper flakes and bring to a boil over high heat. Reduce the heat to low, cover partially, and simmer for 30 minutes.

**3.** Add the clams, cover tightly, and bring to a boil over high heat. Cook until the clams open, about 5 minutes. Discard any clams that do not open. Serve in individual soup bowls, allowing guests to season their soup with a splash of tequila, if desired.

Soaking mussels and clams before cooking helps them expel sand—nothing is worse than biting into a plump clam, only to be greeted by grit. Get into the habit of soaking these mollusks while preparing the other components of the dish. It's easy: rinse and scrub the shellfish under cold running water. Discard any shellfish that feel unnaturally heavy, as they may be filled with sand or mud. If the mussels have their beards attached, pull them off. Place the shellfish in a large bowl and cover with cold water. Stir in about $1/4$ cup cornmeal or flour and 1 tablespoon salt. Let stand for 30 minutes to 1 hour. Drain well.

# Creamy Mussel Chowder with Chipotle Peppers

MAKES 4 TO 6 SERVINGS

I know that Northeastern cooks like their clam chowder—but even dyed-in-the-wool traditionalists will love this souped-up recipe. Chipotle peppers do their magic in waking up a dish that (sometimes) can be just a little *too* comforting.

6 SLICES BACON

1 CUP THINLY SLICED SCALLIONS, WHITE AND GREEN PARTS

1 POUND RED-SKINNED POTATOES, SCRUBBED, UNPEELED, AND CUT INTO ½-INCH CUBES

1 CUP BOTTLED CLAM JUICE

1 WHOLE CANNED CHIPOTLE PEPPER, FINELY CHOPPED, WITH 1 TEASPOON ADOBO (SAUCE)

2 POUNDS MUSSELS, SCRUBBED AND SOAKED

½ CUP HEAVY CREAM

SALT AND FRESHLY GROUND BLACK PEPPER

**1.** In a Dutch oven or flameproof casserole, cook the bacon over medium heat until crisp and brown, about 5 minutes. Transfer the bacon to paper towels to drain. Crumble the bacon and set aside.

**2.** Pour off all but 2 tablespoons fat from the Dutch oven. Add the scallions and cook until softened, about 3 minutes. Add the potatoes, 1 cup cold water, clam juice, and chipotle and adobo. Bring to a boil and reduce the heat to medium. Cover tightly and cook until the potatoes are barely tender, about 20 minutes.

**3.** Add the mussels and crumbled bacon and bring the liquid to a boil over high heat. Cover tightly and cook, shaking the pot occasionally, until the mussels open, about 5 minutes. Add the heavy cream and bring just to a boil. Season with the salt and pepper (you may not need any, as the mussels are naturally salty, and the chipotles are spicy). Serve in deep soup bowls.

Don't remove the beards from mussels more than 2 hours before cooking. If the beards are slippery, use a kitchen towel or even pliers to help grasp them. Farm-raised mussels don't have beards. If you have the time, soak the mussels before using (see page 38).

# Shrimp and Orzo Cioppino

MAKES 6 SERVINGS

Cioppino, a fish and shellfish stew served all over San Francisco, is usually made with crab. We don't get much fresh crab in El Paso, so I make my cioppino with shrimp—and it's hardly a compromise. To make the soup more rib-sticking, I add orzo, a rice-shaped pasta, but you can use any small soup pasta, or even long-grain rice.

1 POUND MEDIUM SHRIMP, PEELED AND DEVEINED, SHELLS RESERVED

1 CUP BOTTLED CLAM JUICE

2 TABLESPOONS OLIVE OIL

1 LARGE ONION, CHOPPED

2 MEDIUM CELERY RIBS WITH LEAVES, CHOPPED

1 MEDIUM RED BELL PEPPER, SEEDED AND CHOPPED

2 GARLIC CLOVES, MINCED

1 CUP HEARTY RED WINE, SUCH AS ZINFANDEL

ONE 28-OUNCE CAN TOMATOES IN JUICE, DRAINED, JUICES RESERVED, AND CHOPPED

1 TEASPOON DRIED BASIL

1 TEASPOON DRIED OREGANO

1 BAY LEAF

½ TEASPOON SALT, PLUS MORE TO TASTE

¼ TEASPOON CRUSHED HOT RED PEPPER FLAKES

⅓ CUP ORZO

**1.** In a medium saucepan, bring the shrimp shells, clam juice, and 1½ cups cold water to a simmer over medium heat. Reduce the heat to low and partially cover. Simmer for 15 minutes. Strain through a wire sieve into a medium bowl. You should have 3 cups—add water, if needed. Set the stock aside.

**2.** Meanwhile, in a Dutch oven or flameproof casserole, heat the oil over medium heat. Add the onion, celery, red pepper, and garlic. Cook, stirring occasionally, until the vegetables soften, about 5 minutes. Add

the wine, bring to a boil, and cook until reduced to ½ cup, about 3 minutes. Add the reserved stock, tomatoes with their juices, the basil, oregano, bay leaf, salt, and red pepper flakes. Simmer for 20 minutes. Stir in the orzo and cook until almost, but not quite, tender, about 8 minutes.

**3.** Add the shrimp and cook until pink and firm, about 3 minutes. Discard the bay leaf. Serve in deep soup bowls.

# fish and shellfish main courses

MORE AND MORE, PEOPLE ARE APPRECIATING FISH FOR ITS MANY BENEFITS. NOT ONLY IS fish good for you, but it cooks quickly, allowing the cook to get a tasty meal on the table in minutes. As the interest in fish increases, different varieties are showing up at fish markets across the country.

El Paso is not San Diego. We do not have fish fresh off the boat at our markets. The fish is as fresh as it can be, but the selection isn't enormous. When I thought about what recipes to share in this chapter, I decided it would be most helpful to other cooks if I used the varieties I call "real fish," instead of exotica.

When you think about how much the market for fish has changed in the last few years (can you imagine walking into your corner market ten years ago and finding fresh tuna steaks?), it looks like the situation will improve. While most fish comes filleted or cut into steaks, these cuts are easier and quicker to cook . . . and no one in my family likes looking at a whole fish, anyway. Farm-raised fish has also made a big difference in how we buy fish. Aquaculture has made fish more abundant and less expensive.

Fish should be kept as cold as possible until serving. It's a good idea to keep it on ice—just place the fish, wrapped in a plastic bag, on a bed on ice in a dish in the refrigerator. As the ice melts, replace it. If you bring live shellfish like mussels or clams home from the market, store them in paper bags, as they will suffocate in plastic bags. Keep them refrigerated, but don't store on ice.

Some of these fish dishes are marinated. Do not overmarinate fish, or the acids in the marinade will "cook" the fish and turn it into seviche. Seviche is delicious, but it isn't grilled fish.

# Flounder in Three-Mushroom Sauce

Flounder is on the mild side, and benefits from being matched with bold flavors. This three-mushroom sauce fits the bill with three mushrooms, Marsala wine, and an enriching splash of cream.

½ CUP DRY MARSALA

1 CUP (¾ OUNCE) DRIED PORCINI MUSHROOMS

2 TABLESPOONS UNSALTED BUTTER

8 OUNCES CREMINI (BABY PORTOBELLO) MUSHROOMS, THINLY SLICED

8 OUNCES WHITE BUTTON MUSHROOMS, THINLY SLICED

3 TABLESPOONS MINCED SHALLOTS

½ TEASPOON DRIED THYME

½ CUP HEAVY CREAM

½ TEASPOON SALT

⅛ PLUS ¼ TEASPOON FRESHLY GROUND BLACK PEPPER

FOUR 6-OUNCE FLOUNDER FILLETS

3 TABLESPOONS ALL-PURPOSE FLOUR

*GARNISH:* CHOPPED FRESH PARSLEY

**1.** In a small saucepan, bring the Marsala and ¹/₂ cup water to a boil over high heat. Add the dried porcini and remove from the heat. Let stand until the porcini soften, about 20 minutes. Lift the mushrooms out of the soaking liquid, chop coarsely, and set aside. Strain the liquid through a paper towel–lined wire sieve into a small bowl and set aside.

**2.** In a large (12-inch) nonstick ovenproof skillet set over medium heat, melt the butter. Add the cremini and white mushrooms and cook, stirring occasionally, until the mushrooms give off their juices, about 3 minutes. Add the chopped porcini and the strained soaking liquid. Cook until the liquid evaporates, about 5 minutes more. Stir in the shallots and thyme and cook until the shallots soften, about 2 minutes. Stir in the cream. Season with ¹/₄ teaspoon salt and ¹/₈ teaspoon pepper.

**3.** Season the fillets with the remaining ¹/₄ teaspoon salt and ¹/₄ teaspoon pepper. Starting at a short end, roll up each fillet into a thick roulade. Place in the skillet and cover tightly. Reduce the heat to medium-low and simmer until the flounder looks opaque when pierced in the center, 10 to 12 minutes. Sprinkle with the parsley and serve immediately.

**Variation:**

For a lighter version of this dish, substitute milk for the cream. After cooking the shallots, sprinkle the mushroom mixture with 2 teaspoons flour and stir for 30 seconds. Stir in the milk and bring to a simmer.

# Pecan-Crusted Catfish with Lemon-Jalapeño Drizzle

MAKES 4 TO 6 SERVINGS

Today's catfish is farm-raised and delicately flavored, and doesn't taste like the muddy-flavored ones from Dad's fishing trips. If you are just too stubborn to give the new catfish a try, make this recipe with perch or snapper fillets.

2 TABLESPOONS ALL-PURPOSE FLOUR

1½ TABLESPOONS CAJUN SEASONING (SEE BELOW)

¼ TEASPOON SALT

1 LARGE EGG

2 TABLESPOONS MILK

¾ CUP FINELY CHOPPED PECANS

FOUR 6-OUNCE CATFISH FILLETS

2 TABLESPOONS VEGETABLE OIL

2 TABLESPOONS UNSALTED BUTTER

1 SCALLION, WHITE AND GREEN PARTS, MINCED

1 JALAPEÑO PEPPER, SEEDED AND MINCED

1 GARLIC CLOVE, MINCED

3 TABLESPOONS FRESH LEMON JUICE

**1.** Position a rack in the top third of the oven and pre-heat to 350°F. In a shallow dish, mix the flour, Cajun seasoning, and salt. In another shallow dish, mix the egg and milk. Place the pecans on a dinner plate. Dip each piece of catfish in the flour, then in the egg mixture, and then in the pecans, pressing the pecans to adhere.

**2.** In a large (12-inch) nonstick ovenproof skillet (wrap the handle with aluminum foil to protect it in the oven, if necessary), heat the oil over medium-high heat. Add the fillets and reduce the heat to medium. Cook until the underside is toasted, about 3 minutes. Turn the fillets. Place the skillet in the oven and bake until the centers of the fillets look opaque when flaked with the tip of knife, 5 to 7 minutes.

**3.** Transfer the fish fillets to dinner plates. Add the butter to the skillet and heat over high heat. Add the scallion, jalapeño, and garlic. Cook, stirring almost constantly, until softened, about 1 minute. Add the lemon juice and drizzle equal amounts over the fillets. Serve immediately.

Choose a relatively salt-free Cajun seasoning (Paul Prudhomme is a good brand, but others are mostly salt with a few spices). To make your own seasoning, mix 1 tablespoon sweet Hungarian paprika, 1 teaspoon each dried thyme and dried basil, $^1/_2$ teaspoon each onion powder, garlic powder, and freshly ground black pepper, and $^1/_4$ teaspoon cayenne pepper. Store leftover Cajun seasoning in a small jar in a dark, cool place, and use as a seasoning for grilled meats and poultry. Makes about $2^1/_2$ tablespoons.

# Park's Salmon Teriyaki

MAKES 4 SERVINGS

One of my favorite suppers is broiled salmon, brushed with a thick teriyaki glaze, then served on top of a heap of Ginger-Sesame Spinach. Quick, classy, and a ginger lover's dream.

2 TABLESPOONS UNSULFURED MOLASSES

2 TABLESPOONS SOY SAUCE

2 TEASPOONS FRESHLY SQUEEZED GINGER JUICE
   (SEE PAGE 9)

FOUR 7-OUNCE SALMON FILLETS

1 RECIPE GINGER-SESAME SPINACH (PAGE 153)

**1.** Position a rack 6 inches from the source of heat and preheat the broiler. Lightly oil a broiler pan.

**2.** In a shallow glass baking dish, mix the molasses, soy sauce, and ginger juice. Place the salmon in the dish, turn to coat, and let stand for 30 minutes.

**3.** Broil the salmon, skin side down, until it is done to your liking, about 4 minutes for medium (with a slightly rosy center).

**4.** Divide the spinach equally among 4 dinner plates, and top each with a salmon fillet. Serve immediately.

# Grilled Salmon Salad Niçoise

MAKES 8 SERVINGS

Cooking the salmon this way creates a crisp, blackened skin that I love. A whole side of salmon is fun to grill like this—it looks impressive on top of a big platter of colorful greens, garnished with cherry tomatoes and grilled potatoes. However, cut it into individual portions before grilling, if you think they will be easier to handle. The top of the fillet is spread with an unusual sour cream and mustard glaze to help keep the fish from drying out.

**LEMON MUSTARD VINAIGRETTE**

2 TABLESPOONS RED WINE VINEGAR

2 TABLESPOONS FRESH LEMON JUICE

2 TABLESPOONS MINCED SHALLOTS

1 TABLESPOON DIJON MUSTARD

GRATED ZEST OF 1 LEMON

1 TEASPOON SUGAR

½ TEASPOON SALT

¼ TEASPOON FRESHLY GROUND BLACK PEPPER

¾ CUP EXTRA-VIRGIN OLIVE OIL

**TO COMPLETE THE RECIPE**

ONE 3½- TO 4-POUND SALMON FILLET IN 1 PIECE

⅓ CUP SOUR CREAM

⅓ CUP DIJON MUSTARD

2 TABLESPOONS CHOPPED FRESH DILL OR
GREEN PART OF A SCALLION

½ TEASPOON FRESHLY GROUND BLACK PEPPER

10 CUPS MESCLUN OR OTHER MIXED SALAD GREENS

1 RECIPE GRILLED NEW POTATOES IN GARLICKY MUSTARD
CRUST (PAGE 150)

2 CUPS CHERRY TOMATOES, PREFERABLY BOTH YELLOW
AND RED

**1.** To make the vinaigrette, whisk together all of the ingredients except the oil in a medium bowl. Gradually whisk in the oil until the vinaigrette thickens. Set aside.

**2.** Using a pair of tweezers, feel over the cut surface of the salmon and remove any small bones. (Sterilize the tweezers first by holding over an open flame for a few seconds.) In a small bowl, mix the sour cream, mustard, dill, and pepper.

**3.** Build a charcoal fire in an outdoor grill and let the coals burn until covered with white ash. Let the coals burn medium-hot. You should be able to hold your hand over the coals at grate level for 3 to 4 seconds. (Or preheat a gas grill on high, then adjust to medium.) Oil the grilling grate well to discourage the skin from sticking. Spread the mustard mixture over the cut surface of the salmon fillet. Place the salmon skin side down and cover. Grill until the skin is crisp and blackened, and the flesh looks barely opaque when prodded with a knife in the thickest part, 15 to 20 minutes.

4. Place the mesclun on a large platter and toss with the dressing. Using 2 large spatulas, transfer the salmon to the platter. Spoon the potatoes around the salmon. Sprinkle with the cherry tomatoes. To serve, cut the salmon vertically into portions, transfer to dinner plates, and serve with a heap of salad and potatoes on the side.

The secret of good grilling is to control the fire. Certain foods cook best if they are seared over high heat, and others are better if they are cooked more slowly over medium heat. Of course, with a gas grill, this can be accomplished with the twist of a dial. With a charcoal fire, the longer it burns, the cooler it eventually becomes. Also, the fire will burn faster and hotter if the air vents are opened wide to allow the maximum amount of oxygen into the grill (fires need air to live, just like humans). And hardwood charcoal chunks burn hotter than charcoal briquettes.

First, build the fire and let the coals burn until they are covered with white ash. This will take about twenty minutes. To gauge the heat of your charcoal fire, hold your hand just above the cooking grate. If the fire is hot (good for steaks and burgers), you should be able to hold your hand over the grill for only 1 or 2 seconds. If you let the fire burn down to medium (preferred for more delicate meats, fish, and poultry), you should be able to stand the heat for only about 3 seconds before you start cursing me for telling you how to do this. Don't cook your hand!

# Swordfish Soft Tacos with Guaca-Salsa-Mole

MAKES 8 SERVINGS

Just about every Mexican restaurant in San Diego offers a version of fish tacos, and they are a delicious addition to taco repertoire. This recipe only looks long—it's really quite easy—because I've included a recipe for a chunky avocado salsa.

**FOR THE SWORDFISH**

½ CUP FRESH LIME JUICE

2 TEASPOONS GROUND MILD CHILE PEPPER,
    SUCH AS CHIMAYO

1 GARLIC CLOVE, MINCED

¼ TEASPOON SALT

¼ CUP OLIVE OIL

1 LARGE ONION, THINLY SLICED

2½ POUNDS SWORDFISH STEAKS, CUT ½ INCH THICK,
    SKIN REMOVED

**FOR THE GUACA-SALSA-MOLE**

1 LARGE RIPE BEEFSTEAK TOMATO, SEEDED AND
    CHOPPED INTO ½-INCH CUBES

1 LARGE RIPE HASS AVOCADO, PITTED, PEELED, AND
    CHOPPED INTO ½-INCH CUBES

1 JALAPEÑO PEPPER, SEEDED AND MINCED

2 TABLESPOONS MINCED RED ONION

1 TABLESPOON FRESH LIME JUICE

¼ TEASPOON SALT

**TO COMPLETE THE RECIPE**

2 TABLESPOONS OLIVE OIL

1 LARGE ONION, THINLY SLICED

1 GARLIC CLOVE, MINCED

EIGHT 6-INCH CORN TORTILLAS

2 CUPS SHREDDED ROMAINE LETTUCE LEAVES

CILANTRO LEAVES, FOR SERVING

HOT RED PEPPER SAUCE, FOR SERVING

**1.** To marinate the swordfish, whisk together the lime juice, ground chile, garlic, and salt in a medium bowl. Whisk in the oil. Add the onion. Transfer to a large self-sealing plastic bag. Add the swordfish and seal the bag. Refrigerate, turning occasionally, for at least 15 minutes and up to 2 hours, no longer.

**2.** To make the guaca-salsa-mole, combine all the ingredients in a medium bowl Cover with a piece of plastic wrap, pressing the wrap directly on the surface. Set aside until ready to serve.

**3.** Meanwhile, heat the oil in a large skillet over

medium heat. Add the onion and cook, stirring occasionally, until well softened and browned, about 10 minutes. Stir in the garlic and cook until fragrant, about 30 seconds. Reheat before using.

**4.** Build a charcoal fire in an outdoor grill and let the coals burn until they are covered with white ash and medium-hot. You should be able to hold your hand at grate level for 3 seconds. Or preheat a gas grill on high, then reduce to medium. Lightly oil the grill grate. Remove the fish from the marinade. Place the fish on the grill and cover. Grill, turning once, until the fish is

just opaque when pierced in the center, about 6 minutes. Transfer to a cutting board and coarsely chop into $1/2$-inch cubes. In a medium bowl, mix the fish with the warm onion mixture and cover with foil to keep warm.

**5.** Place the tortillas on the grill and cook, turning once, until warm, lightly toasted, and flexible, about 30 seconds. Wrap them in a towel to keep warm. Serve the tortillas and fish, allowing guests to make their own tacos, adding guaca-salsa-mole, lettuce, cilantro, and hot pepper sauce to taste.

# Tuna and Zucchini Kebabs with Orange-Tarragon Marinade

MAKES 4 SERVINGS

Tuna's inherent meatiness makes it a good match for this thick tarragon-scented marinade with hints of orange, lemon, and tomato. It can be tricky to get all of the food on a kebab done at the same time, so parboil the zucchini first.

**FOR THE MARINADE**

⅓ CUP FRESH ORANGE JUICE

3 TABLESPOONS OLIVE OIL

2 TABLESPOONS FRESH LEMON JUICE

2 TABLESPOONS TOMATO PASTE

1 TABLESPOON SOY SAUCE

1 TEASPOON DRIED TARRAGON

2 GARLIC CLOVES, CRUSHED THROUGH A PRESS

¼ TEASPOON CRUSHED HOT RED PEPPER FLAKES

**TO COMPLETE THE RECIPE**

1½ POUNDS TUNA, CUT INTO SIXTEEN 1½-INCH CUBES

1 MEDIUM ZUCCHINI, CUT LENGTHWISE, THEN CROSSWISE INTO 12 PIECES

4 LONG BAMBOO SKEWERS, SOAKED FOR 30 MINUTES IN WATER AND DRAINED

**1.** To make the marinade, whisk together all of the ingredients in a shallow glass baking dish until smooth. Add the tuna and toss to coat with the marinade. Cover and refrigerate for at least 20 minutes but no longer than 2 hours.

**2.** Bring a large pot of lightly salted water to a boil over high heat. Add the zucchini and cook for 1 minute. Drain and rinse under cold running water. Set aside.

**3.** Build a hot charcoal fire in an outdoor grill and let burn until the coals are covered with white ash. You should be able to hold your hand at grate level for only 1 to 2 seconds. (Or preheat a gas grill on high.) Lightly oil the grill.

**4.** Add the zucchini to the marinade and toss to coat. Thread 4 pieces of tuna and 3 pieces of zucchini onto each skewer. Grill, turning occasionally, until cooked to desired doneness, about 8 minutes for medium-rare. Serve hot.

# Tuna au Poivre with Port Sauce

You've heard of steak *au poivre*, where steaks are crusted with cracked peppercorns, but tuna takes well to the *au poivre* treatment, too.

FOUR 6-OUNCE TUNA STEAKS, SKIN REMOVED,
   CUT ABOUT ¾ INCH THICK

2 TEASPOONS OLIVE OIL

1½ TEASPOONS COARSELY CRACKED PEPPERCORNS
   (CRUSHED IN A MORTAR OR UNDER A HEAVY SKILLET)

¼ TEASPOON SALT

3 TABLESPOONS UNSALTED BUTTER

2 TABLESPOONS CHOPPED SHALLOTS

1 CUP TAWNY OR RUBY PORT

1½ TEASPOONS CHOPPED FRESH ROSEMARY, OR
   ½ TEASPOON DRIED

SALT AND FRESHLY GROUND BLACK PEPPER

**1.** Position a rack in the center of the oven and preheat to 200°F. Brush the tuna steaks with the olive oil. Press equal amounts of the cracked pepper all over each tuna steak and season with the salt.

**2.** Heat a large (12-inch) nonstick skillet over medium-high heat. Add the tuna and cook, turning once, until seared on both sides, about 3 minutes total for medium-rare tuna. Transfer to a baking sheet and keep warm in the oven while making the sauce.

**3.** Add 1 tablespoon butter to the skillet and melt over medium heat. Add the shallots and stir until softened, about 30 seconds. Add the port and rosemary. Bring to a boil over high heat. Cook until reduced to about ⅓ cup, 3 to 4 minutes. Remove from the heat and swirl in the remaining 2 tablespoons butter to thicken the sauce. Season lightly with salt and pepper. Serve the tuna on individual dinner plates, and top each with a spoonful of sauce.

# Scallops and Asparagus au Gratin

A big dish of tender scallops and fresh asparagus in wine sauce, topped with a crunchy bread crumb coating, is what I make to treat myself well.

1 POUND ASPARAGUS, WOODY STEMS DISCARDED,
   CUT INTO 1-INCH LENGTHS
1½ CUPS CHICKEN BROTH, PREFERABLY HOMEMADE, OR
   USE LOW-SODIUM CANNED BROTH
⅓ CUP DRY WHITE WINE, SUCH AS CHARDONNAY
1½ POUNDS SEA SCALLOPS
3 TABLESPOONS UNSALTED BUTTER
2 TABLESPOONS CHOPPED SHALLOTS
3 TABLESPOONS ALL-PURPOSE FLOUR

⅓ CUP MILK
1 TEASPOON CHOPPED FRESH TARRAGON, OR
   ½ TEASPOON DRIED
¼ TEASPOON SALT
⅛ TEASPOON FRESHLY GROUND WHITE PEPPER
¾ CUP FRESH BREAD CRUMBS (SEE OPPOSITE PAGE)
¼ CUP FRESHLY GRATED PARMESAN CHEESE
*GARNISH:* 2 TABLESPOONS CHOPPED FRESH PARSLEY
   (OPTIONAL)

**1.** Position a broiler rack 6 inches from the source of heat and preheat the broiler. Lightly butter a flame-proof 13 × 9-inch baking dish.

**2.** Bring a medium saucepan of lightly salted water to boil over high heat. Add the asparagus and cook until crisp-tender, about 3 minutes. Drain and set aside. (Do not rinse the asparagus.)

**3.** In a medium saucepan, bring the broth and wine to a boil over high heat. Add the scallops and cook just until the scallops are opaque, about 3 minutes. (The liquid does not have to return to a boil.) Using a slot-ted spoon, transfer the scallops to the prepared dish and set aside. Scatter the asparagus over the scallops.

**4.** In another medium saucepan, melt 2 tablespoons butter over medium heat. Add the shallots and cook, stirring often, until softened, about 2 minutes. Sprinkle with the flour and stir well. Reduce the heat to low and cook without browning, stirring often, for 2 minutes. Add the cooking liquid, milk, and tarragon and bring to a simmer. Simmer over medium-low heat until thickened and no trace of flour taste remains, about 5 minutes. Season with the salt and pepper.

**5.** Pour over the scallops and asparagus. Sprinkle with the bread crumbs and cheese and dot with small pieces of the remaining 1 tablespoon butter. Broil until the topping is browned, about 1 minute. Serve immediately, sprinkled with parsley.

Homemade bread crumbs are a versatile ingredient and are used for everything from topping casseroles to breading chicken. They're easy to make. Just place day-old bread slices (French, Italian, or firm sandwich bread with or without crusts) in a food processor fitted with a metal blade, and process until they form crumbs. You can also make the crumbs in small batches in a blender. I keep a stash of bread crumbs in a self-sealing plastic bag stored in the freezer. Some recipes that need fine bread crumbs use dried bread crumbs from the supermarket, but get the unflavored variety.

# Steamed Shrimp with Cajun Spices

MAKES 4 SERVINGS

Steamed shrimp is one of the simplest of all supper dishes. It goes like this: Place seasoned shrimp over simmering liquid, cover, and cook for a few minutes, then roll up your sleeves and eat. Instead of the familiar Old Bay seasoning from the East Coast, I go to the Bayou country for inspiration. Serve this with corn on the cob and potato salad.

2 POUNDS MEDIUM SHRIMP, UNPEELED

1½ TABLESPOONS CAJUN SEASONING (SEE PAGE 46)

**1.** Place a metal collapsible steamer in a large saucepan. Pour enough water into the saucepan to reach ⅛ inch from the bottom of the steamer. Cover tightly and bring to a boil over high heat.

**2.** Layer the shrimp in the steamer, sprinkling liberally with the spice mixture. Cover tightly and steam until the shrimp are pink and firm, 3 to 5 minutes. Spoon the shrimp into individual bowls and serve hot, peeling the shrimp at the table and encouraging everyone to lick the spices from their fingers.

# Grilled Shrimp with
# Guava Barbecue Glaze

Guava paste is an important ingredient in Puerto Rican cooking, and is easy to find in Hispanic markets. It is simple to transform this perfumed paste into a delicious marinade for peeled shrimp that glazes the shrimp perfectly during grilling. If you like, alternate chunks of fresh pineapple on the skewers with the shrimp.

**FOR THE GLAZE**
1 TABLESPOON UNSALTED BUTTER
¼ CUP MINCED ONION
1 GARLIC CLOVE, MINCED
⅔ CUP GUAVA PASTE
2 TABLESPOONS CIDER VINEGAR
2 TABLESPOONS DIJON MUSTARD
1 TABLESPOON SOY SAUCE

⅛ TEASPOON SALT
⅛ TEASPOON HOT PEPPER SAUCE

**TO COMPLETE THE RECIPE**
2 POUNDS LARGE SHRIMP
BAMBOO SKEWERS, SOAKED FOR 30 MINUTES IN WATER,
    THEN DRAINED

**1.** To make the glaze, heat the butter in a small saucepan over medium heat. Add the onion and garlic and cover. Cook, stirring occasionally, until the onion is golden, about 4 minutes. Stir in the guava paste, vinegar, mustard, soy sauce, salt, and hot pepper sauce. Cook, stirring constantly, just until the guava paste is melted. Cool completely. Whisk in ¼ cup water.

**2.** In a large, heavy-duty, self-sealing plastic bag, combine the shrimp and the glaze. Refrigerate, turning occasionally, for at least 15 minutes and up to 2 hours, no longer.

**3.** Meanwhile, build a charcoal fire in an outdoor grill and let it burn until the coals are covered with white ashes. Let it burn until medium-hot. You should be able to hold your hand at grill level for about 3 seconds. (Or preheat a gas grill to medium.) Lightly oil the grill.

**4.** Drain the shrimp. Skewer the shrimp on the bamboo skewers. Cover the grill and cook until the shrimp are glazed and begin to turn opaque around the edges, about 3 minutes. Turn and continue grilling just until the shrimp are pink and firm, 2 to 3 minutes. Serve immediately.

# poultry main courses

WHEN FRANCE'S HENRY IV HOPED THAT EVERYONE WOULD EVENTUALLY HAVE A CHICKEN in the pot for Sunday dinner, I doubt he ever imagined that, almost five hundred years later, many Americans would be eating chicken almost every night!

Chicken has always been a versatile bird, as at home in the pot as on the grill or in a skillet. Being able to buy chicken parts means that you can get your favorite portion. And boneless and skinless chicken breasts have got to be the most popular single cooking ingredient of the 1990s, at least with my circle of friends. While people cook a lot of chicken, very few do it right. The two most common mistakes are overcooking and overmarinating.

When I warn against overcooked chicken, don't worry—I'm not going to promote raw chicken sushi. But too often, chicken gets overcooked in the face of concerns about bacteria in the kitchen, which is a culinary case of throwing the baby out with the bathwater. When cooking chicken, an instant-read thermometer could be your best buddy. If you have any doubts about your chicken being cooked, place the thermometer in the thickest part of the bird (or chicken part), not touching the bone. In a whole roasted chicken, the ideal place for taking the temperature is the thigh. Chicken is thoroughly cooked, but not dried out, at 170°F. You can also cut into the chicken with a sharp knife at the thigh and be sure that there is no sign of pink near the bone, but you can lose precious juices this way. Also, if you do pierce the cooked chicken, those juices should run clear yellow, with no sign of pink.

It is especially important to avoid overcooking boneless and skinless chicken breasts. These are usually cooked through in 10 to 12 minutes. The best way to tell if chicken breast is done is to press it in the center—it should feel firm and spring back. If you wish, cut into the center of the breast to be sure it is cooked through and opaque white. But as soon as it reaches that state, take it off the fire, or you will think you are eating shoe leather instead of chicken breast.

Marinating chicken overnight seems like a good idea. If you get a lot of flavor by marinating for 2 hours, I think most people believe they'll get twelve times the flavor if they let it soak for 24 hours. Well, it just ain't so. One of these days, taste a piece of marinated meat or chicken at its center. I'll bet you'll see that the marinade penetrated only about $1/8$ inch around the outside, something that is accomplished with a 2-hour soak. But most important, over-marinating changes the texture of chicken, just as it does fish. If your marinade has strong flavors and includes acidic ingredients like wine, citrus juice, or vinegar, you don't need to marinate the chicken longer than 2 hours, or the chicken might "cook" in the marinade, and have a cottony texture after grilling.

# Perfect Roast Chicken

The typical 4-pound bird really doesn't go very far when you want roast chicken. Call the butcher and order a good-sized roasting chicken (if the market doesn't already carry them). With a little restraint at suppertime, you may even have leftovers. In my opinion, the less you do to a roast chicken, the better, the more to savor its old-fashioned flavor.

ONE 6½-POUND CHICKEN, GIBLETS RESERVED FOR
   ANOTHER USE
2 TABLESPOONS EXTRA-VIRGIN OLIVE OIL
SALT AND FRESHLY GROUND BLACK PEPPER
1 SMALL ONION, CHOPPED
1 SMALL CARROT, CHOPPED

2 GARLIC CLOVES, MINCED
¼ TEASPOON DRIED THYME
2 TABLESPOONS MINCED SHALLOT
APPROXIMATELY 1⅔ CUPS CHICKEN BROTH, PREFERABLY
   HOMEMADE, OR USE LOW-SODIUM CANNED BROTH
2 TABLESPOONS CHILLED UNSALTED BUTTER

**1.** Rinse the chicken and pat completely dry with paper towels. Let stand at room temperature for 30 minutes to 1 hour before roasting.

**2.** Position a rack in lower third of the oven and pre-heat to 400°F. Rub the chicken all over with oil. Season inside and out with the salt and pepper. Fold the wings akimbo behind the chicken's back or tie them loosely to the body with kitchen string. Place the onion, carrot, garlic, and thyme in the chicken cavity. Don't bother to close the cavity or truss the chicken. Place the chicken on one side on a lightly oiled adjustable roasting rack in a roasting pan, with wing facing up.

**3.** Roast the chicken for 20 minutes. Remove from the oven. Spoon off any clear yellow fat, leaving the brown drippings in the pan. Stick a large metal spoon in the cavity (a wooden spoon may break), protect the other hand with a pot holder or folded kitchen towel, and turn the chicken to the other side. Roast for 20 minutes more. Remove from the oven, adjust the rack to the flat position, and place the chicken on its back on the rack. Continue roasting until a meat thermometer inserted in thickest part of thigh registers 175°F, about 1 hour. (Calculate total roasting time by using weight of chicken *without* giblets, allowing approximately 18 minutes per pound.) Remove from the oven, transfer to a serving platter, and let stand for 10 minutes.

**4.** Pour the pan juices into a glass measuring cup. Add juices from chicken cavity. Let stand 5 minutes.

Skim the yellow fat from the surface, reserving 1 tablespoon, leaving juices in cup. Place the roasting pan on 2 stove burners over medium heat. Add reserved fat and the shallot. Cook, stirring often, until shallot is translucent, about 2 minutes. Add enough broth to degreased juices to make 2 cups. Pour into the pan and bring to a boil over high heat. Boil until reduced to about 3/4 cup, about 8 minutes. Remove from heat. One tablespoon at a time, whisk in the butter until melted. Season with salt and pepper. Carve the chicken and serve with the sauce.

What makes a roast chicken perfect? It has a evenly browned, crisp, golden skin—most easily achieved by turning the chicken during roasting so the heat reaches all areas. Let the chicken stand at room temperature for at least 30 minutes before cooking (so it roasts evenly), and then let it stand for at least 10 minutes before carving (so the juices simmering inside the bird redistribute themselves).

# Rosemary Chicken on Tomato and Bread Salad

MAKES 4 TO 6 SERVINGS

This is a chicken dish for diners who get bored easily, as every bite is different from the next.

6 TABLESPOONS EXTRA-VIRGIN OLIVE OIL

2 GARLIC CLOVES, CRUSHED UNDER A KNIFE

4 CUPS (ABOUT 10 OUNCES) DAY-OLD ITALIAN OR
   FRENCH BREAD, CUT INTO ¾-INCH CUBES

ONE 4-POUND CHICKEN, CUT INTO 8 PIECES

2 TABLESPOONS FRESH LEMON JUICE

1 TABLESPOON CHOPPED FRESH ROSEMARY

1 TEASPOON SALT, PLUS MORE TO TASTE

½ TEASPOON CRUSHED HOT RED PEPPER FLAKES

¼ CUP BALSAMIC VINEGAR

½ CUP CHICKEN BROTH, PREFERABLY HOMEMADE, OR
   USE CANNED LOW-SODIUM BROTH

FRESHLY GROUND BLACK PEPPER

8 CUPS MESCLUN OR OTHER MIXED SALAD GREENS

2 MEDIUM BEEFSTEAK TOMATOES, SEEDED AND
   CUT INTO ¾-INCH CUBES

2 TABLESPOONS CHOPPED FRESH BASIL

2 TABLESPOONS CHOPPED FRESH PARSLEY

**1.** Position a rack in the top third of the oven and preheat to 375°F. In a small saucepan, heat 2 tablespoons of the oil and the garlic over medium heat until the garlic is sizzling but not browned, about 3 minutes. Using a slotted spoon, discard the garlic. In a large bowl, toss the bread cubes with the garlic oil. Arrange on a baking sheet. Bake, tossing occasionally, until the cubes are golden, about 15 minutes. Set the bread cubes aside.

**2.** Lightly oil a large roasting pan. In a large bowl, toss the chicken with 2 tablespoons oil, the lemon juice, rosemary, salt, and red pepper flakes. Arrange the chicken in a single layer in the roasting pan. Roast the chicken, turning occasionally, until it shows no sign of

pink when pierced at the bone, about 45 minutes. Transfer the chicken to a platter, tent with aluminum foil to keep warm, and set aside.

**3.** Pour off the fat and place the pan over high heat on top of the stove. Add the vinegar, broth, and remaining 2 tablespoons oil and bring just to a boil, scraping up any browned bits in the pan. Season to taste with salt and pepper. Set the dressing aside.

**4.** To serve, place the mesclun on a large serving platter. Top with the bread cubes, scatter the tomatoes over the cubes, and sprinkle with the basil and parsley. Drizzle with the dressing. Top with the chicken and serve immediately.

# Grilled Chicken with Lemon-Herb Rub

When you want well-seasoned grilled chicken, but don't have the time to soak it in marinade, give it a massage with herbs, olive oil, and lemon zest, and get cooking! Cooking the chicken by the indirect method reduces flareups (the chicken drips around the coals, not onto them to feed a flame) and works like a dream.

ONE 4-POUND CHICKEN, CUT INTO 8 PIECES

2 TABLESPOONS EXTRA-VIRGIN OLIVE OIL

GRATED ZEST OF 1 LEMON

1 TEASPOON DRIED ROSEMARY

1 TEASPOON DRIED BASIL

1 TEASPOON DRIED OREGANO

1 TEASPOON SALT

½ TEASPOON CRUSHED HOT RED PEPPER FLAKES

LEMON WEDGES, FOR SERVING

**1.** Build a hot charcoal fire in an outdoor grill and let burn until covered with white ash. You should be able to hold your hand at grate level for only 1 to 2 seconds. Or preheat one side of a gas grill on high, leaving the other burner(s) off. Lightly oil the grill.

**2.** Rinse the chicken and pat dry with paper towels. In a small bowl, mix the oil, lemon zest, rosemary, basil, oregano, salt, and red pepper flakes. Rub the paste all over the chicken.

**3.** Leave the ignited charcoal heaped in a mound in the center of the grill—do not spread out the coals. Place the chicken around the outside perimeter of the grill, not directly over the coals. (For gas grill, place on the turned-off areas.) Cover and grill, turning the chicken 2 or 3 times during cooking, until the chicken shows no sign of pink when pierced at a bone, about 45 minutes. Serve with the lemon wedges.

# Cassoulet, Italian-Style

MAKES 6 SERVINGS

Few dishes warm the insides like cassoulet. While the dish comes originally from southwestern France, my version is seasoned with an Italian hand. It has also been trimmed down in both the amount of time needed to pull the cassoulet together and in the amount of fat it usually serves up. Serve this with a green salad, and you'll have a great supper for taking the chill off a cold winter's night.

2 TABLESPOONS OLIVE OIL

6 CHICKEN THIGHS (2¼ POUNDS TOTAL)

8 OUNCES SWEET ITALIAN PORK OR TURKEY SAUSAGE, CASINGS REMOVED

1 MEDIUM ONION, CHOPPED

2 GARLIC CLOVES, MINCED

½ TEASPOON DRIED THYME

½ TEASPOON DRIED ROSEMARY

½ TEASPOON DRIED SAGE

½ TEASPOON DRIED OREGANO

½ TEASPOON SALT

¼ TEASPOON FRESHLY GROUND BLACK PEPPER

ONE 16-OUNCE CAN TOMATOES, JUICES RESERVED, CHOPPED

½ CUP CHICKEN BROTH, PREFERABLY HOMEMADE, OR USE LOW-SODIUM CANNED BROTH

½ CUP DRY WHITE WINE, SUCH AS CHARDONNAY

1 BAY LEAF

6 CUPS COOKED WHITE BEANS (CANNELLINI), OR THREE 15½-OUNCE CANS, DRAINED AND RINSED

½ CUP DRIED UNFLAVORED BREAD CRUMBS

2 TABLESPOONS CHOPPED FRESH PARSLEY

**1.** Position a rack in the center of the oven and preheat to 375°F. Lightly oil a deep 3½-quart baking dish or ovenproof casserole.

**2.** In a large skillet, heat 1 tablespoon of the oil over medium-high heat. Rinse the chicken and pat dry with paper towels. Add the chicken thighs, skin side down, and cook, turning once, until browned on both sides, about 6 minutes. Transfer to a plate and set aside.

**3.** Pour off all but 1 tablespoon of the fat in the skillet. Add the sausage and cook, stirring to break up the sausage with the side of a spoon, until seared but not browned, about 5 minutes. Pour off all but 1 tablespoon of the fat. Add the onion and garlic and cook, stirring occasionally, until the onion softens, about 3 minutes. Add the thyme, rosemary, sage, oregano, salt, and pepper. Stir in the tomatoes with their juices, the broth, wine, and bay leaf. Bring to a simmer.

4. Transfer the sauce to the prepared dish and stir in the beans. Bury the chicken thighs in the beans. Sprinkle with the bread crumbs and parsley, then drizzle with the remaining 1 tablespoon oil. Bake for 20 minutes. Using the back of a large spoon, press the crumb topping just under the surface of the cassoulet. Bake until the cassoulet is bubbling and a deep golden crust has formed on top, about 30 minutes. Let stand for 5 minutes. Serve hot, removing the bay leaf when serving.

# El Paso Arroz con Pollo

MAKES 4 TO 6 SERVINGS

Around here, everyone has a recipe for chicken and rice. It's the kind of dish that personifies "supper": easy to make, comforting to eat. My formula gets a kick with spicy chorizo sausage and a little jalapeño pepper thrown in for good measure.

3 OUNCES SMOKED CHORIZO LINKS, CASINGS REMOVED, CUT INTO ¼-INCH CUBES

6 CHICKEN THIGHS (2¼ POUNDS TOTAL)

½ TEASPOON SALT

¼ TEASPOON FRESHLY GROUND BLACK PEPPER

1 MEDIUM ONION, CHOPPED

1 MEDIUM RED BELL PEPPER, SEEDED AND CHOPPED

1 JALAPEÑO PEPPER, SEEDED AND MINCED

2 GARLIC CLOVES, MINCED

1½ CUPS LONG-GRAIN RICE

2½ CUPS CHICKEN BROTH, PREFERABLY HOMEMADE, OR USE LOW-SODIUM CANNED BROTH

½ CUP DRY WHITE WINE, SUCH AS CHARDONNAY

1 TEASPOON DRIED OREGANO

⅛ TEASPOON CRUMBLED SAFFRON THREADS, OR ¼ TEASPOON TURMERIC

1 CUP THAWED FROZEN PEAS

**1.** Position a rack in the center of the oven and preheat to 350°F. In a large (12-inch) ovenproof skillet, cook the chorizo with ½ cup water over high heat until the water evaporates and the chorizo is sizzling, about 5 minutes. Using a slotted spoon, transfer the chorizo to a plate and set aside.

**2.** Rinse the chicken and pat dry with paper towels. Place the chicken in the skillet, skin side down, and reduce the heat to medium. Cook, turning once, until the chicken is browned on both sides, about 8 minutes. Season with ¼ teaspoon salt and the pepper. Transfer to the plate with the chorizo. Pour out all but 1 tablespoon of the fat from the skillet.

**3.** Add the onion, red pepper, jalapeño, and garlic. Cook, stirring occasionally, until softened, about 5 minutes. Add the rice and cook, stirring occasionally, until it turns translucent, about 2 minutes. Add the broth, wine, oregano, saffron, and remaining ¼ teaspoon salt. Return the chicken and the chorizo to the skillet. Bring to a boil over high heat.

**4.** Cover tightly and bake until the chicken is cooked through and the rice is tender, about 25 minutes. Top with the peas, recover, and let stand for 5 minutes. Serve immediately.

Many of my recipes call for white wine, which is always in our refrigerator at home. I cook with the same simple, dry white wine that I like to drink. It doesn't have to be expensive, just tasty. There are a lot of Californian, Australian, and Chilean wines that fall into this category. While I recommend chardonnay, try sauvignon blanc, too. Unless the recipe specifies it, stay away from semi-dry wines like riesling.

# Chile-Stuffed Chicken Breasts

Roasted chiles and cheese are a great pair and make a terrific stuffing for chicken breasts. To save time, I use canned mild chiles, but if you want to grill, peel, and seed a poblano or Anaheim chile, go ahead—but you may end up with more chile than you need. Keep the chile-mayonnaise topping in mind for whenever you need a simple brush-on to spice up any grilled chicken parts or fish steaks. Serve with Parmesan Polenta (page 149).

6 CHICKEN BREAST HALVES, WITH SKIN AND BONES
   (ABOUT 9 OUNCES EACH)
3 OUNCES SHARP CHEDDAR CHEESE, THINLY SLICED
ONE 4-OUNCE CAN MILD GREEN CHILES, DRAINED, SPLIT
   LENGTHWISE TO MAKE 6 LARGE STRIPS TOTAL

¾ CUP MAYONNAISE
3 TABLESPOONS FRESH LIME JUICE
4 TEASPOONS CHILI POWDER
3 GARLIC CLOVES, CRUSHED THROUGH A PRESS

**1.** Build a charcoal fire on one side of an outdoor grill. Or preheat gas grill on high. Turn one burner off and adjust the other burner(s) to high.

**2.** Using a small, sharp knife, cut deep pockets into the meaty part of each breast. Stuff each pocket with some of the cheese and 1 piece of chile. Close each pocket with wooden toothpicks. In a small bowl, mix the mayonnaise, lime juice, chili powder, and garlic; set aside.

**3.** Place the chicken breasts, skin side down, on the side of the grill opposite the coals. If using a gas grill, place over the turned-off area. Brush generously with the mayonnaise mixture. Cover and grill for 15 minutes. Turn the chicken and brush with the remaining mayonnaise mixture. Cover and continue grilling until the chicken shows no sign of pink when pierced at the bone, about 15 minutes. Serve hot.

# Oven-Fried Chicken Nuggets with Salsa Dip

MAKES 4 SERVINGS

If you have kids, you know how they love crispy chicken nuggets from the local fast-food joint. The homemade version is much better tasting, and fun to make. Dip them in whatever strikes your fancy. We like the salsa dip at my house, but sometimes bottled barbecue sauce hits the spot, too.

1½ POUNDS BONELESS AND SKINLESS CHICKEN BREASTS

1½ CUPS FRESH BREAD CRUMBS, PREPARED IN A
  BLENDER FROM FRENCH OR ITALIAN BREAD
  (SEE PAGE 55)

½ CUP FRESHLY GRATED PARMESAN CHEESE

1 TABLESPOON CHILI POWDER

1 TEASPOON DRIED OREGANO

¼ TEASPOON GARLIC POWDER

¼ TEASPOON SALT

⅓ CUP MILK

2 TABLESPOONS OLIVE OIL

1 CUP PREPARED SALSA, DRAINED TO REMOVE
  EXCESS LIQUID

½ CUP SOUR CREAM

**1.** Position a rack in the top third of the oven and preheat to 400°F. Lightly oil a 15 × 10 × 1-inch jelly roll pan.

**2.** Rinse the chicken, pat dry, and cut into 1-inch pieces. In a medium bowl, combine the bread crumbs, Parmesan cheese, chili powder, oregano, garlic powder, and salt. Place the milk in another medium bowl. A few pieces at a time, dip the chicken in the milk, then coat with the crumb mixture and place on the prepared pan.

**3.** Drizzle with the oil. Bake, turning halfway through baking, until the nuggets are golden and show no sign of pink when pierced in the center, about 20 minutes.

**4.** In a medium bowl, mix the drained salsa and sour cream. Divide the dipping sauce into individual small bowls or custard cups. Serve the nuggets with the dipping sauce.

# Chicken-Fried Chicken Breasts with Sassy Buttermilk Gravy

## MAKES 4 SERVINGS

Fried chicken is certainly in the Supper Hall of Fame. Here's an updated, quick version, with a tangy, spicy sauce for lavishing onto a heap of mashed potatoes. Try to let the coated breasts stand for a while before cooking—this will keep the delicious crunchy coating intact. If you're not a buttermilk fan, use all milk for the gravy, but still use buttermilk for dipping the breasts, and keep any remaining buttermilk on hand for baking.

FOUR 6-OUNCE BONELESS AND SKINLESS CHICKEN
    BREASTS
1/2 CUP PLUS 1/3 CUP BUTTERMILK
1 TEASPOON HOT PEPPER SAUCE, SUCH AS TABASCO,
    PLUS MORE TO TASTE
1 CUP ALL-PURPOSE FLOUR

1/2 TEASPOON SALT, PLUS MORE TO TASTE
1/4 TEASPOON FRESHLY GROUND BLACK PEPPER
VEGETABLE OIL, FOR FRYING
2/3 CUP MILK
1/2 TEASPOON CHILI POWDER

**1.** Using the flat side of a meat mallet, gently pound the chicken breasts to an even thickness. In a pie plate, mix 1/2 cup buttermilk and 1 teaspoon hot pepper sauce. (Let the remaining 1/3 cup buttermilk stand at room temperature so it loses its chill.) In another pie plate or shallow dish, mix the flour, 1/2 teaspoon salt, and 1/4 teaspoon pepper. One at a time, dip the chicken breasts in the spiced buttermilk, then coat with the flour and place on a wire cake rack over a baking sheet. Reserve 1 1/2 tablespoons of the seasoned flour. Refrigerate the chicken for 30 minutes to 1 hour to set the coating.

**2.** In a large skillet, heat enough oil to come 1/4 inch up the sides over medium-high heat until very hot but not smoking. Add the chicken breasts and cook, turning halfway through cooking, until golden brown, 12 to 15 minutes. Adjust the heat as needed so the chicken doesn't brown too quickly. Return to the wire rack to drain.

**3.** Pour the oil into a bowl; return 1 1/2 tablespoons to the skillet over low heat. Whisk in the reserved flour and let bubble for 2 minutes. Whisk in the milk and chili powder and bring to a simmer—the gravy will be thick. Remove from the heat and whisk in the remaining $\frac{1}{3}$ cup buttermilk. Season with salt and hot pepper sauce. Serve the chicken breasts with the sauce passed on the side.

Buttermilk, like sour cream and yogurt, will curdle if heated in a sauce, so it must be stirred in off the heat. If chilled buttermilk is added to a hot sauce, it will cool off the sauce. But if it is at room temperature, the sauce will remain hot.

# Grilled Chicken Breasts
# with Blackberry-Sage Glaze

### MAKES 6 SERVINGS

This wonderful brush-on glaze, with its deep purple color and equally rich flavors of blackberries,
port wine, and chipotle, should be added during the last few minutes of cooking—
don't add it any earlier, or it will scorch.

**FOR THE GLAZE**

¾ CUP BLACKBERRY OR RASPBERRY PRESERVES

2 TABLESPOONS TAWNY OR RUBY PORT WINE

2 TEASPOONS FINELY CHOPPED FRESH SAGE, OR
   1 TEASPOON DRIED

2 TEASPOONS FINELY CHOPPED *CHIPOTLE EN ADOBO*,
   WITH ITS SAUCE

1 TABLESPOON RED WINE VINEGAR

1 TEASPOON SOY SAUCE

**TO CONTINUE THE RECIPE**

SIX 6-OUNCE BONELESS AND SKINLESS CHICKEN BREASTS

1 TABLESPOON OLIVE OIL

½ TEASPOON SALT

¼ TEASPOON FRESHLY GROUND BLACK PEPPER

**1.** To make the glaze, in a medium saucepan, combine the preserves, port, sage, chipotle with its sauce, vinegar, and soy sauce. Bring to a simmer, then reduce the heat to low and cook, stirring, for 5 minutes. Use the glaze while still warm and spreadable; reheat, if needed.

**2.** Build a charcoal fire in an outdoor grill and let burn until covered with white ash and medium-hot. You should be able to hold your hand at grate level for 3 seconds. Or preheat a gas grill on high, and adjust to medium. Lightly oil the grill.

**3.** Using a flat meat mallet, pound the chicken breasts to an even thickness. Brush the breasts with the oil and season with salt and pepper. Cover and grill for 8 minutes, turning halfway through cooking. Continue grilling, turning and brushing often with the glaze, until the breasts show no sign of pink when pierced in the center, about 5 minutes more. Serve hot, with any remaining glaze drizzled over the breasts.

# Chicken and Broccoli Divan Stir-Fry

One of the all-time great chicken casseroles, chicken and broccoli divan, gets a makeover in this quick version—and there's not a can of cream of mushroom soup in sight! Serve this over hot noodles or rice.

¼ CUP ALL-PURPOSE FLOUR

¼ TEASPOON SALT

¼ TEASPOON FRESHLY GROUND BLACK PEPPER

1½ POUNDS BONELESS AND SKINLESS CHICKEN
    BREASTS, CUT INTO 2 × ½-INCH STRIPS

2 TABLESPOONS VEGETABLE OIL

¼ CUP MINCED SHALLOTS OR SCALLIONS,
    WHITE PARTS ONLY

3 CUPS BROCCOLI FLORETS

⅓ CUP DRY VERMOUTH OR WHITE WINE

1 CUP CHICKEN BROTH, PREFERABLY HOMEMADE, OR
    USE LOW-SODIUM CANNED BROTH

⅓ CUP SOUR CREAM

2 TABLESPOONS DIJON MUSTARD

2 TEASPOONS FRESH TARRAGON, OR ¾ TEASPOON DRIED

HOT COOKED NOODLES OR RICE, FOR SERVING

**1.** In a shallow plate, mix the flour, salt, and pepper. Toss the chicken breasts in the flour, shaking off the excess. In a large (12-inch) nonstick skillet, heat 1 tablespoon of the oil over medium-high heat. Add the chicken and cook, turning occasionally, until lightly browned, about 5 minutes. (You may have to do this in 2 batches, adding a little more oil as needed.) Transfer the chicken to a plate and set aside.

**2.** Add the remaining 1 tablespoon oil to the skillet and heat. Add the shallots and stir until softened, about 30 seconds. Add the broccoli and ½ cup water. Increase the heat to high. Cover and cook until the broccoli is just tender, about 4 minutes. Using a slotted spoon, transfer the broccoli to a bowl and set aside. Discard any water in the skillet.

**3.** Return the skillet to the heat and add the chicken breasts. Add the wine, and then the broth, and bring to a simmer. Reduce the heat to low and cook, stirring, for 2 minutes. Stir in the broccoli. Remove the pan from the heat. Stir in the sour cream, mustard, and tarragon. Serve, spooned over hot noodles or rice.

When cooking with wine in a stir-fry, add it to the hot skillet before adding any other liquids. The wine will "explode" when it hits the hot pan, and a lot of the raw alcohol taste will be released in the burst of steam.

# Chinese Chicken and Cashew Stir-Fry with Spicy Orange Sauce

Put on a pot of rice, and if you're a good chopper, you should have this done in about the same time it takes for the rice to cook. It's for the times when you want Chinese food, but can't face another night of take-out. Some people avoid Asian stir-fries because they seem like a lot of work, but when you consider that they are essentially one-pot meals that include meat and veggies, the scales are tipped in their favor. And practice makes perfect.

3 TABLESPOONS SOY SAUCE

1 TABLESPOON PLUS 2 TEASPOONS CORNSTARCH

1 LARGE EGG WHITE

1½ POUNDS BONELESS AND SKINLESS CHICKEN
   BREASTS, CUT INTO 2 × ½-INCH STRIPS

1 CUP CHICKEN BROTH, PREFERABLY HOMEMADE, OR
   USE LOW-SODIUM CANNED BROTH

GRATED ZEST OF ½ ORANGE

¼ CUP FRESH ORANGE JUICE

1 TABLESPOON BALSAMIC VINEGAR

1 TABLESPOON HOISIN SAUCE

1 TABLESPOON ASIAN DARK SESAME OIL

½ TEASPOON CHILI SAUCE WITH GARLIC, OR ¼ TEASPOON
   CRUSHED HOT RED PEPPER FLAKES

3 TABLESPOONS VEGETABLE OIL

1 TABLESPOON GRATED FRESH GINGER (USE THE LARGE
   HOLES OF A CHEESE GRATER)

3 GARLIC CLOVES, MINCED

1 LARGE RED BELL PEPPER, SEEDED AND CUT INTO
   ½-INCH-WIDE STRIPS

ONE 16-OUNCE CAN BABY CORN, DRAINED AND RINSED

1 CUP (4 OUNCES) UNSALTED CASHEWS

HOT COOKED RICE, FOR SERVING

**1.** In a medium bowl, beat 1 tablespoon of the soy sauce, 1 tablespoon cornstarch, and 1 egg white to dissolve the cornstarch. Add the chicken and set aside.

**2.** In a small bowl, combine the broth, orange zest, orange juice, balsamic vinegar, hoisin sauce, sesame oil, chili sauce, the remaining 2 tablespoons soy sauce and 2 teaspoons cornstarch and mix to dissolve the cornstarch. Set the sauce mixture aside.

**3.** Heat a large (12-inch) nonstick skillet over medium-high heat and add 2 tablespoons of the oil. Add the chicken and stir-fry until seared, 3 minutes. Transfer to a plate and set aside.

**4.** Heat the remaining 1 tablespoon oil in the skillet. Add the ginger and garlic and stir-fry until fragrant, about 30 seconds. Add the red pepper and corn and stir-fry until the pepper is crisp-tender, about 2 minutes. Return the chicken to the skillet, with the cashews. Add the sauce mixture and cook until simmering and thickened, about 1 minute. Serve immediately.

# Asian Sweet and Sticky Chicken Wings

MAKES 4 SERVINGS

You've heard of finger-lickin' chicken wings? Well, you'll *have* to lick the delicious sauce from your fingers with these double-cooked wings. First they're baked to get them golden brown, then they're tossed in a skillet to get slicked with sauce. Serve with a mound of white rice and some stir-fried veggies.

3 POUNDS CHICKEN WINGS

1 TEASPOON VEGETABLE OIL

2 GARLIC CLOVES, MINCED

½ CUP PACKED LIGHT BROWN SUGAR

⅓ CUP BALSAMIC VINEGAR

2 TABLESPOONS SOY SAUCE

½ TEASPOON ASIAN CHILI PASTE WITH GARLIC OR CRUSHED HOT RED PEPPER FLAKES

**1.** Preheat the oven to 400°F. Using a large knife or a cleaver, chop each wing between the joints into 3 sections. Discard the wing tips (or save for making chicken broth). Place the wing sections in a large roasting pan.

**2.** Bake, turning halfway through, until tender and golden brown, 50 to 60 minutes. Pour off the fat from the roasting pan.

**3.** In a large (12-inch) nonstick skillet, heat the oil over medium heat. Add the garlic and stir until fragrant, about 30 seconds. Add the brown sugar, balsamic vinegar, soy sauce, and chili paste and bring to a boil over high heat, stirring to dissolve the sugar. Add the chicken wings and boil, turning the wings occasionally in the sauce, until the sauce thickens and coats the wings, about 5 minutes. Serve immediately.

# Turkey Roulades with Jalapeño Jack and Prosciutto

A quick, elegant sauté that is easy enough to throw together for a weeknight supper, yet fancy enough to serve to company.

SIX 4- TO 5-OUNCE TURKEY BREAST CUTLETS

1 THIN SLICE PROSCIUTTO, CUT INTO 6 PIECES

3 OUNCES JALAPEÑO JACK CHEESE, THINLY SLICED

3 TABLESPOONS DRAINED, COARSELY CHOPPED SUN-
    DRIED TOMATOES IN OIL

¼ TEASPOON SALT

⅛ TEASPOON FRESHLY GROUND BLACK PEPPER

1 TABLESPOON OLIVE OIL

1 TABLESPOON UNSALTED BUTTER

2 TABLESPOONS MINCED SHALLOT

¾ CUP DRY WHITE WINE, SUCH AS CHARDONNAY

2 TEASPOONS CHOPPED FRESH SAGE, OR 1 TEASPOON DRIED

**1.** Place the turkey cutlets between sheets of waxed paper sprinkled with water. Using a flat meat mallet, pound the cutlets until about ⅛ inch thick. Discard the waxed paper. In the center of each cutlet, place 1 piece of prosciutto topped with equal amounts of the cheese and sun-dried tomatoes. Fold in the sides of each cutlet slightly to enclose the filling, then roll up into a cylinder and secure with wooden toothpicks. Season with the salt and pepper.

**2.** In a large (12-inch) nonstick skillet, heat the oil over medium heat. Add the turkey roulades and cook, turning occasionally, until browned on all sides, about 10 minutes. Transfer the roulades to a plate.

**3.** Add the butter to the skillet and heat. Add the shallot and cook until softened, about 1 minute. Add the wine and sage and bring to a boil. Return the turkey to the skillet and reduce the heat to low. Cover and simmer until the turkey shows no sign of pink when pierced to the center, about 5 minutes.

**4.** Transfer the roulades to a platter and cover with aluminum foil to keep warm. Boil the sauce over high heat until reduced to 6 tablespoons, about 3 minutes. Pour over the roulades and serve.

**Note:** Turkey breast is very lean, and should be cooked over medium heat to avoid toughening.

# Classic Turkey Pot Pie
# with Scallion Biscuit Topping

MAKES 4 TO 6 SERVINGS

Some folks reserve turkey pot pie as a venue for leftover holiday turkey, but I think it is well worth making from scratch. It's easy to pull together, thanks to the proliferation of turkey parts at the supermarket and a quick biscuit topping.

**FOR THE FILLING**

1 TABLESPOON UNSALTED BUTTER

8 OUNCES THAWED FROZEN WHITE ONIONS

2 MEDIUM CARROTS, CUT INTO ½-INCH-THICK ROUNDS

2¼ CUPS TURKEY OR CHICKEN BROTH, PREFERABLY HOMEMADE, OR USE LOW-SODIUM CANNED CHICKEN BROTH

1 POUND BONELESS AND SKINLESS TURKEY BREAST, CUT INTO 1-INCH CUBES, RINSED UNDER COLD WATER

¼ CUP ALL-PURPOSE FLOUR

¼ CUP MILK

2 TABLESPOONS CHOPPED FRESH PARSLEY

1 BAY LEAF

½ TEASPOON SALT

¼ TEASPOON FRESHLY GROUND WHITE PEPPER

**FOR THE BISCUITS**

2 CUPS ALL-PURPOSE FLOUR

1 TABLESPOON BAKING POWDER

½ TEASPOON SALT

½ CUP UNSALTED BUTTER, CHILLED, CUT INTO ½-INCH PIECES

¾ CUP MILK, APPROXIMATELY

1 SCALLION, WHITE AND GREEN PARTS, MINCED

**1.** Position a rack in the center of the oven and preheat to 400°F. Lightly butter a deep, 3-quart casserole.

**2.** To make the filling, heat the butter in a medium saucepan over medium heat. Add the onions and carrots and cover. Cook until the carrots are crisp-tender, about 5 minutes. Add the broth and bring to a boil. Add the turkey and cook for 2 minutes, skimming off any foam that rises to the surface.

**3.** In a small bowl, whisk the flour and milk into a paste. Whisk about ½ cup of the broth into the paste, and stir back into the saucepan. Add the parsley, bay leaf, salt, and pepper. Cook until simmering and thickened. Transfer to the prepared casserole.

**4.** To make the topping, whisk together the flour, baking powder, and salt in a medium bowl. Using a pastry blender, cut in the butter until the mixture resembles coarse cornmeal with a few pea-size pieces. Stir in enough of the milk just until a soft dough forms—do not overmix. Add the scallion and quickly knead it into the dough, right in the bowl.

**5.** On a lightly floured surface, using floured hands, pat out the dough until $1/2$ inch thick. Using a $2^{1}/_{2}$-inch round cutter, cut out biscuits, gathering up and patting out the scraps until all the dough is used. Place the biscuits on top of the filling.

**6.** Bake until the biscuits are golden brown, 25 to 30 minutes. Remove bay leaf when serving and serve hot.

# Duck Breasts with Asian Pear Salsa

Many butchers now carry Muscovy duck breasts, sometimes called *magrets*. They are larger than those from the typical Long Island duck, and one breast makes a good-sized serving. They aren't cheap, but when you want to treat yourself special and enjoy duck without the trouble of roasting, duck breasts deliver in a big way. Starting the duck breasts off in a cold pan renders the fat and leaves a crisp, golden skin.

**ASIAN PEAR SALSA**

2 MEDIUM ASIAN PEARS, PEELED, CORED, AND
    CUT INTO ¼-INCH DICE
2 TABLESPOONS MINCED SHALLOT
2 TABLESPOONS FRESH LIME JUICE
1 TABLESPOON HONEY
1 JALAPEÑO PEPPER, SEEDED AND MINCED
2 TEASPOONS CHOPPED FRESH CILANTRO OR MINT

**TO COMPLETE THE RECIPE**

FOUR 10- TO 12-OUNCE BONELESS DUCK BREASTS
    (*MAGRETS*), TRIMMED OF EXCESS SKIN
¼ TEASPOON SALT
¼ TEASPOON FRESHLY GROUND BLACK PEPPER
⅔ CUP CHICKEN BROTH, PREFERABLY HOMEMADE, OR
    USE LOW-SODIUM CANNED CHICKEN BROTH
2 TABLESPOONS UNSALTED BUTTER

**1.** To make the salsa, combine the Asian pears, shallot, lime juice, honey, and jalapeño in a small bowl. Cover and let stand until ready to serve, up to 2 hours. Just before serving, stir in the cilantro.

**2.** Using a sharp knife, score the duck skin in a diamond pattern, being sure not to reach down to the meat. Season with the salt and pepper. Place the breasts, skin side down, in a large (12-inch), cold nonstick skillet. Cook over medium heat, removing the rendered fat with a bulb baster as it accumulates in the skillet, until the skin is golden-brown, about 10 minutes. Turn the breasts and continue cooking until the undersides are lightly browned and the breasts are medium-rare, about 2 more minutes. Transfer to a serving plate, cover with foil to keep warm, and let stand for 2 minutes.

**3.** Pour out any fat in the skillet, leaving the browned bits in the pan. Place the skillet over high heat. Add the broth, stirring up the browned bits with a wooden spon. Boil until reduced to ½ cup, about 2 minutes. Remove from the heat and stir in the butter to slightly thicken the sauce.

4. To serve, slice each duck breast on the bias into thick slices. Place a duck breast on each dinner plate, fanning out the slices. Spoon the sauce over the breasts and serve with the pear salsa.

Duck breast is usually served medium-rare, at which point it has a flavor and texture reminiscent of a fine beef steak. If you'd like your duck breast more well done, be warned that the texture and flavor will change, and not for the better, in my opinion.

# meat main courses

I BELIEVE THAT THE BACKYARD WAS INVENTED TO PROVIDE A HOME FOR THE OUTDOOR grill. Like many red-blooded American males, I am in my element when cooking a sizzling steak over glowing coals (or a piping-hot gas grill). I wish I could explain why men love grilling so much. There must be a scientific explanation. One of these days, some anthropologist is going to do a study and find out a direct sociological link between a guy grilling burgers in his backyard and early man tossing mastodon steaks on hot rocks. Then I can say that I'm not just making supper, but I'm getting in touch with my roots! Or maybe an enterprising genetics expert will *finally* discover that men have a "barbecue" gene (and lack the "doing the dishes" gene).

With the advent of the gas grill, people are grilling year-round, not just during the summer. (Most gas grills have two cooking units, right and left. However, one of most popular gas grills, the Weber, has three burners that go front-middle-back. My gas grill instructions work for both types.) I truly believe that you can cook just about anything on the grill (although my experiment with pasta didn't go too well). If you are a city dweller and don't have a grill, translate the grilled recipes for your broiler. Position the broiler rack about 6 inches from the source of heat. Preheat the broiler for at least 10 minutes to get it good and hot before cooking. The recipes will take about the same amount of time, or a few minutes longer. Some grilling recipes call for indirect heat (where the food is placed next to, but not over, the coals, and cooked by radiating heat), so the food will cook through without burning. If you want to cook these recipes in a broiler, don't worry about adjusting, because a broiler is much cooler than a grill.

# Grilled Sirloin Steaks with Lemon-Pepper Rub

Grilled steaks have an allure that the fanciest cooking can't surpass. If you get your hands on dry-aged steaks from a good butcher, you don't have to do a thing to them—just season with salt and pepper and grill, baby, grill. But most of us can only get supermarket steaks that could use a little fixing up. This easy lemon zest, cracked pepper, and garlic rub does the trick. Sear the steak over hot coals, then continue cooking by the indirect heat method to ensure that the garlic in the rub doesn't scorch and get bitter.

6 GARLIC CLOVES

1 TEASPOON SALT

GRATED ZEST OF 2 LARGE LEMONS (2 TEASPOONS)

1 TEASPOON COARSELY CRACKED BLACK PEPPERCORNS
(CRUSHED IN A MORTAR OR UNDER A HEAVY SKILLET)

1 TABLESPOON VEGETABLE OIL

FOUR 12-OUNCE SHELL OR SIRLOIN STEAKS,
CUT ABOUT 1 INCH THICK

**1.** On a work surface, chop the garlic. Sprinkle with the salt, and chop and mash until it forms a paste. Sprinkle with the lemon zest and pepper, and continue chopping until well combined. Scrape up, transfer to a small bowl, and stir in the oil.

**2.** Rub the paste on both sides of the steaks. Let stand at room temperature for up to 30 minutes while preparing the grill.

**3.** Build a hot charcoal fire in an outdoor grill, and let the coals burn until they are covered with white ash. Bank the coals to one side of the grill and spread evenly. Or preheat a gas grill on high. Turn one burner off and keep the other burner(s) on high. Lightly oil the grill. Grill the steaks over the coals, covered, until seared, about 2 minutes. Turn and sear the other side, another 2 minutes. Move the steaks to the empty (off) side of the grill. Cover and continue cooking until the steaks are medium-rare, about 6 minutes. Serve hot.

If you like your steaks "blackened" with a crusty exterior, do not rub the steaks with the lemon-pepper mixture before grilling. Grill the steaks directly over the coals (or heating element on high) until cooked to your desired doneness (about 6 minutes for medium-rare), then smear the rub onto the steaks just before serving.

To tell the doneness of steaks, press in the middle with a finger. Rare steaks feel soft, medium steaks have some spring, but well-done are firm.

# Flank Steak with Pico de Gallo Marinade

This quickly made marinade changes character with whatever salsa is used. Best is a chunky refrigerated kind, often called *pico de gallo*, but a high-quality bottled salsa is fine, too.

1 CUP LAGER BEER

1 CUP FRESH PREPARED SALSA,
     PREFERABLY *PICO DE GALLO* (SEE NOTE)

2 TABLESPOONS FRESH LIME JUICE

½ TEASPOON SALT

ONE 2-POUND FLANK STEAK, WELL TRIMMED

**1.** Mix the beer, salsa, and lime juice in a 15 × 10-inch glass baking dish. Add the flank steak and cover. Let stand at room temperature at least 30 minutes or up to 1 hour, turning occasionally. (Or refrigerate for up to 8 hours, removing from the refrigerator 1 hour before grilling.)

**2.** Build a charcoal fire in an outdoor grill and let burn until covered with white ash. (Or preheat a gas grill on high.) Lightly oil the grill grate. Remove the flank steak from the marinade, but do not wipe off any clinging bits of marinade. Season the steak with the salt. Grill the steak, covered, turning once, until medium-rare, about 8 minutes.

**3.** Transfer the steak to a carving board, cover loosely with aluminum foil to keep warm, and let stand for 3 minutes. Using a sharp carving knife held at a 45-degree angle, cut the steak into thin slices. Serve with the juices poured over the steak.

**Note:** To make your own *pico de gallo*, mix 1 cup seeded, chopped ripe plum tomatoes, 3 tablespoons minced white onion, 2 tablespoons fresh lime juice (in addition to the lime juice in the marinade), 1 seeded and minced jalapeño pepper, 1 minced garlic clove, and 2 tablespoons chopped fresh cilantro (optional). Season with salt to taste.

Flank steaks should be cooked no more than medium-rare, or they will toughen. They are never very thick, and if the steak is cooked while cold from the refrigerator, it could still be cold in the center even after grilling. So be sure the flank steak has been out of the refrigerator for at least 30 minutes and up to 1 hour before tossing onto the grill. And let the steak stand for a couple of minutes before slicing—it will be juicier.

# Spiced-Rubbed Beef Tenderloin Kebabs

MAKES 4 SERVINGS

Spice rubs deliver Texas-sized flavor without marinating. Beef tenderloin makes the best kebabs because they don't need a liquid soak to tenderize.

1 TEASPOON CUMIN SEEDS, COARSELY CRACKED IN A MORTAR

1 TEASPOON CORIANDER SEEDS, COARSELY CRACKED IN A MORTAR

1 TEASPOON DRIED OREGANO

½ TEASPOON SALT

½ TEASPOON COARSELY CRACKED BLACK PEPPERCORNS (CRUSHED IN A MORTAR OR UNDER A HEAVY SKILLET)

1 POUND BEEF TENDERLOIN, CUT INTO 1-INCH CUBES

3 TABLESPOONS EXTRA-VIRGIN OLIVE OIL

8 MEDIUM WHITE MUSHROOM CAPS

1 SMALL ONION, QUARTERED, THEN HALVED LENGTHWISE TO MAKE 8 WEDGES

1 TABLESPOON FRESH LEMON JUICE

1 TABLESPOON SOY SAUCE

**1.** In a medium bowl, mix the cumin, coriander, oregano, salt, and peppercorns. In another medium bowl, toss the beef cubes with 1 tablespoon oil. Place the beef in the spices and toss to coat.

**2.** Thread the beef cubes onto skewers with the mushrooms and onion wedges. In a small bowl, mix the remaining 2 tablespoons oil with the lemon juice and soy sauce. Set the kebabs and soy-lemon mixture aside.

**3.** Build a charcoal fire in an outdoor grill and let burn until covered with white ash. (Or preheat a gas grill on high.) Lightly oil the grill grate. Grill the kebabs, covered, turning and basting occasionally with the soy-lemon mixture, until the beef is medium-rare, about 8 minutes. Serve hot.

# Salsa Meat Loaf

MAKES 4 TO 6 SERVINGS

If meat loaf is good, meat loaf with salsa in it is *great*! This is the Cadillac of meat loaves, ready to serve next to a mountain of mashed potatoes. If you like to have gravy with your spuds, I've included an easy one for your pleasure (see below).

1 CUP PREPARED SALSA, LIGHTLY DRAINED TO REMOVE
   EXCESS LIQUID

½ CUP UNFLAVORED DRY BREAD CRUMBS

⅓ CUP MINCED ONION

1 LARGE EGG, BEATEN

1 TEASPOON SALT

½ TEASPOON GROUND CUMIN

8 OUNCES GROUND ROUND (15% LEAN) BEEF

8 OUNCES GROUND PORK

8 OUNCES GROUND VEAL

2 TABLESPOONS TOMATO PASTE

**1.** Position a rack in the center of the oven and preheat to 375°F. In a large bowl, mix the salsa, bread crumbs, onion, egg, salt, and cumin. Add the ground round, pork, and veal, and mix with your hands just until combined. Transfer to a 9 × 5-inch loaf pan.

**2.** Place the loaf pan on a baking sheet. Bake for 1¼ hours. Spread the tomato paste over the top of the meat loaf and continue baking until a meat thermometer inserted in the center of the meat loaf reads 165°F, about 10 minutes more. Remove from the oven and let stand for 5 minutes before serving. Serve hot.

**Meat Loaf Gravy:** Drain the fat from the cooked meat loaf into a small bowl. Transfer 2 tablespoons of fat to a small saucepan and heat over medium-low heat. Whisk in 2 tablespoons of all-purpose flour and cook until lightly browned, about 2 minutes. Whisk in 1 cup beef broth (preferably homemade or use low-sodium canned broth) and bring to a boil over medium heat. Reduce the heat to low and simmer for 5 minutes. Season with salt and pepper.

# Pot Roast with New Mexican Chile Sauce

MAKES 6 SERVINGS

The New Mexico chiles in this pot roast make a thick, dark red sauce to spoon over Parmesan Polenta (page 149) or hot noodles. Be sure to buy mild New Mexico chiles, unless you live with a family of fire-eaters.

10 NEW MEXICO OR OTHER MILD WHOLE DRIED CHILES, RINSED, SPLIT, STEMMED, AND SEEDED

2 CUPS BOILING WATER

ONE 6-OUNCE CAN TOMATO PASTE

ONE 28-OUNCE CAN PEELED TOMATOES, CHOPPED, WITH JUICES

4 TABLESPOONS OLIVE OIL

ONE 3-POUND BEEF CHUCK ROAST

½ TEASPOON SALT

¼ TEASPOON FRESHLY GROUND BLACK PEPPER

1 LARGE ONION, CHOPPED

2 MEDIUM CARROTS, CUT INTO 1-INCH LENGTHS

3 GARLIC CLOVES, MINCED

1 TABLESPOON DRIED OREGANO

2 TEASPOONS CUMIN SEEDS, TOASTED AND CRUSHED (PAGE 107)

1 POUND MEDIUM RED-SKINNED POTATOES, SCRUBBED BUT UNPEELED, CUT INTO 1-INCH CUBES

**1.** In a medium bowl, soak the chiles in the water until softened, about 20 minutes. Drain, reserving ¼ cup of the soaking liquid. Transfer the soaked chiles, tomato paste, tomatoes with their juices, and the reserved soaking liquid to a blender and puree. Set the puree aside.

**2.** Preheat the oven to 300°F. In a large, heavy-bottomed Dutch oven, heat 3 tablespoons of the oil over medium-high heat. Add the roast and cook, turning once, until browned on both sides, about 10 minutes. Transfer to a plate, season with the salt and pepper, and set aside.

**3.** Add the remaining 1 tablespoon oil to the pot and reduce the heat to medium. Add the onion, carrots, and garlic and cook until the onion is softened, about 4 minutes. Stir in the tomato-chile puree, oregano, and cumin. Return the roast with its juices to the pot and bring the sauce to a boil. Cover and bake for 2 hours. Add the potatoes and cook until the meat is fork-tender, about 1 hour more.

**4.** Transfer the pot roast to a large, deep platter and tent with aluminum foil to keep warm. Let the sauce stand for 5 minutes. Skim off and discard the fat from the surface of the sauce. Spoon the vegetables and sauce around the pot roast and serve.

# Grilled Beef Ribs
# with Hoisin Glaze

MAKES 4 SERVINGS

Beef spareribs (don't confuse them with short ribs) are delectable. Like pork ribs, they remind me of a line from a Tracy-Hepburn movie, where Spencer says of Katharine: "She don't have much meat on her, but what there is, is *choice*!" Allow about 1 pound of ribs per person, or more if they don't seem meaty enough. The grilled ribs are finished off with a slightly sweet sauce—like many brush-ons, remember that it can burn easily, so don't use it too early.

4 POUNDS BEEF SPARERIBS

½ TEASPOON SALT

¼ TEASPOON FRESHLY GROUND BLACK PEPPER

2 TEASPOONS VEGETABLE OIL

2 TABLESPOONS GRATED FRESH GINGER (USE THE LARGE HOLES OF A BOX GRATER)

3 GARLIC CLOVES, CRUSHED THROUGH A PRESS

½ CUP CATSUP

½ CUP HOISIN SAUCE

3 TABLESPOONS DRY SHERRY

1 TABLESPOON RICE VINEGAR

1 TABLESPOON SOY SAUCE

**1.** Build a charcoal fire in an outdoor grill and let burn until the charcoal is covered with white ash. Or preheat a gas grill on high. Turn one burner off, then adjust the other burner(s) to low. Season the beef lightly with the salt and pepper and set aside.

**2.** In a medium saucepan, heat the oil over medium-high heat. Add the ginger and garlic and stir until fragrant, about 1 minute. Stir in the remaining ingredients and bring to a simmer. Reduce the heat to low and simmer for 1 minute. Remove the sauce from the heat.

**3.** Lightly oil the grill grate. If using charcoal, do not spread out the coals; leave them heaped in a mound in the center. Grill the ribs over the coals, turning occasionally, until well browned, about 10 minutes. Move to the cooler area of the grill, around the coals (not over them), cover, and grill, turning occasionally until tender, 15 to 20 minutes more. Return them to the hot area over the coals, and grill, turning and basting often with the sauce, until the ribs are glazed, about 5 minutes. If using a gas grill, brown over the hot areas, then move to the low areas, and return to the hot areas for glazing.

# Short Ribs with Beer and Horseradish Sauce

I've hardly met a beef stew I didn't like, but when they're made with short ribs, I get downright lustful. The meat on the bone is especially succulent, and the bones add body to the sauce. Horseradish gives this stew a slow-burn kind of sizzle.

2 TABLESPOONS VEGETABLE OIL

6 MEATY SHORT RIBS (ABOUT 4½ POUNDS)

1 TEASPOON SALT

¼ TEASPOON FRESHLY GROUND BLACK PEPPER

1 LARGE ONION, CHOPPED

3 MEDIUM CARROTS, CUT INTO ½-INCH ROUNDS

3 MEDIUM CELERY RIBS, CUT INTO ¼-INCH-THICK SLICES

4 GARLIC CLOVES, MINCED

¼ CUP ALL-PURPOSE FLOUR

2 CUPS BEEF BROTH, PREFERABLY HOMEMADE, OR USE LOW-SODIUM CANNED BROTH

1 CUP LAGER BEER

1 TABLESPOON TOMATO PASTE

1 TEASPOON CARAWAY SEEDS

1 TEASPOON DRIED THYME

1 BAY LEAF

2 TABLESPOONS PREPARED HORSERADISH

**1.** Position a rack in the center of the oven and pre-heat to 300°F. In a large Dutch oven or flameproof casserole, heat the oil over medium-high heat. In batches, add the short ribs and cook, turning occasion-ally, until browned, about 10 minutes. Transfer to a plate and season with the salt and pepper.

**2.** Add the onion, carrots, celery, and garlic to the pot. Cook over medium heat, stirring often, until the onion is golden, about 10 minutes. Sprinkle with the flour and stir well. Whisk in the broth, beer, tomato paste, caraway seeds, thyme, and bay leaf. Return the short ribs with their juices to the pot and bring to a simmer.

**3.** Bake, covered, until the short ribs are tender, about 2½ hours. Transfer the short ribs to a deep serving platter and cover with aluminum foil to keep warm. Let the sauce stand for 5 minutes. Skim off the fat from the surface of the sauce and discard the bay leaf. Stir in the horseradish. Spoon the sauce and vegetables over the short ribs and serve immediately.

# Crown Roast of Pork with Cranberry-Sausage Stuffing and Bourbon Gravy

### MAKES 8 TO 12 SERVINGS

I can hear you thinking: Isn't crown roast of pork too complicated for supper? The hardest part about this recipe is ordering the roast from the butcher. It's just two pork loins tied together into a ring with a center that cries out for a wonderful stuffing like this one studded with dried cranberries. Serve it for a big Sunday supper with friends.

**FOR THE STUFFING**

2 TABLESPOONS VEGETABLE OIL

1 LARGE ONION, CHOPPED

2 MEDIUM CELERY RIBS WITH LEAVES, CHOPPED

2 JALAPEÑO PEPPERS, SEEDED AND MINCED

2 GARLIC CLOVES, MINCED

2 POUNDS GROUND PORK (WILL OFTEN COME WITH
    THE CROWN ROAST OF PORK)

1 CUP WELL-CRUSHED CORNBREAD OR
    REGULAR STUFFING MIX

3 LARGE EGGS, BEATEN

⅓ CUP CHOPPED FRESH PARSLEY

2 TEASPOONS DRIED SAGE

1 TEASPOON DRIED ROSEMARY

2 TEASPOONS SALT

¾ TEASPOON FRESHLY GROUND BLACK PEPPER

1 CUP DRIED CRANBERRIES

1 CUP SHELLED PISTACHIOS OR SLIVERED ALMONDS

**TO COMPLETE THE RECIPE**

ONE 8½-POUND CROWN ROAST OF PORK,
    CONSISTING OF 14 RIBS

1 TEASPOON SALT

½ TEASPOON CRUMBLED DRIED SAGE

½ TEASPOON DRIED ROSEMARY

½ TEASPOON DRIED THYME

½ TEASPOON FRESHLY GROUND BLACK PEPPER

2 TABLESPOONS VEGETABLE OIL

3 CUPS BEEF BROTH, PREFERABLY HOMEMADE, OR
    USE LOW-SODIUM CANNED BROTH

4 TEASPOONS CORNSTARCH

3 TABLESPOONS BOURBON OR THAWED FROZEN APPLE JUICE
    CONCENTRATE

**1.** To make the stuffing, heat the oil in a large skillet over medium heat. Add the onion, celery, jalapeño peppers, and garlic. Cook, stirring, until the onion is golden, about 6 minutes. Transfer to a large bowl. Add the ground pork, crushed cornbread stuffing, eggs, parsley, sage, rosemary, salt, and pepper and mix well. Mix in the dried cranberries and pistachios.

**2.** Position a rack in the bottom third of the oven and preheat the oven to 450°F. Place the roast in a roasting pan just large enough to hold it comfortably. In a small bowl, combine the salt, sage, rosemary, thyme and pepper. Brush the roast with the oil, then season all over with the herb mixture. Fill the center of the roast with the stuffing. Protect the stuffing by covering the center portion with piece of aluminum foil. Cover each of the bone tips with a small piece of foil.

**3.** Bake the roast for 10 minutes. Reduce the oven temperature to 325°F. Cook until a meat thermometer inserted in the thickest part of the roast, without touching a bone, reads 155°F, about 2 hours. During the last 15 minutes of cooking time, remove the foil from the stuffing and bone tips to allow them to brown. Using a wide spatula (or a rimless baking sheet, or even the flat round bottom of a tart pan), transfer the roast to a warmed serving platter. Let the roast stand for 10 minutes before carving.

**4.** Meanwhile, discard any fat in the roasting pan. Place the pan over 2 stove burners at medium-high heat. Add the broth and bring to a boil, scraping up any browned bits on the bottom of the pan. In a small bowl, dissolve the cornstarch in the bourbon. Whisk into the broth and cook until boiling and lightly thickened. Pour the sauce into a warmed sauceboat.

**5.** Using a long, sharp knife, starting at the center of the stuffing, cut the roast and stuffing into 2-rib servings (or 1-rib servings for lighter eaters). Serve with the sauce passed on the side.

Because you have to transfer the roast and stuffing intact from the roasting pan to a platter, the butcher will usually provide a disposable tray to contain and support the roast. If the butcher neglects to do this, just place the roast on the removable flat bottom from a large tart pan. Or place the roast on an oiled round of aluminum foil. Move the roast to the platter on the foil, then carefully slide the foil out from underneath the roast.

# Roast Pork Tenderloin with Pomegranate Sauce

## MAKES 4 SERVINGS

Pomegranates are one of autumn's glories, and their juice makes a wonderful tart sauce to brush onto grilled pork. You might be wondering how to get the juice out of those pomegranates, but don't worry—it's easy, and you don't have to have an electric juicer to do it. This should be served with the Orange and Pomegranate Salad on page 17.

### FOR THE POMEGRANATE SAUCE

2 POMEGRANATES

2 TABLESPOONS OLIVE OIL

1 SMALL ONION, CHOPPED

1 GARLIC CLOVE, MINCED

2 TABLESPOONS BALSAMIC VINEGAR

2 TEASPOONS CHOPPED FRESH ROSEMARY, OR
   ½ TEASPOON DRIED

⅛ TEASPOON SALT

⅛ TEASPOON FRESHLY GROUND BLACK PEPPER

### TO COMPLETE THE RECIPE

TWO 12-OUNCE PORK TENDERLOINS, THIN ENDS FOLDED
   BACK AND TIED WITH KITCHEN STRING

1 TABLESPOON OLIVE OIL

¼ TEASPOON SALT

¼ TEASPOON FRESHLY GROUND BLACK PEPPER

**1.** To make the sauce, first juice the pomegranates: Using a small knife, cut a shallow *X* in the top of each pomegranate through its protruding blossom end. Fill a large bowl with water. Submerge a pomegranate in the water, and pull open the *X* to break each pomegranate into quarters. (This will keep the juice from splattering all over you and the kitchen.) With the pomegranate still submerged, work the seeds from the yellow pith—the seeds will sink to the bottom. Discard the skin when the seeds are removed. Repeat with the other pomegranate. Skim off any pith floating on the surface, and drain the seeds in a wire sieve placed over a bowl. Using a large spoon, press on the seeds to release the juice. You should have 2 cups.

**2.** In a medium saucepan, heat the oil over medium heat. Add the onion and garlic and cook until softened, about 3 minutes. Add the pomegranate juice, balsamic vinegar, and rosemary and bring to a boil over high heat. Boil until reduced by half, about 10 minutes. Season with the salt and pepper and set aside.

**3.** Meanwhile, build a charcoal fire in an outdoor grill and let burn until covered with white ash. Or preheat a gas grill on high. Lightly oil the grill grate. Brush the tenderloins with the oil and season with the salt and pepper. Grill the tenderloins, turning occasionally, until browned on all sides, about 10 minutes. Continue grilling and turning, brushing often with about half of the pomegranate sauce, until the tenderloins are glazed and an instant-read thermometer inserted in their centers reads 150°F, about 10 minutes more.

**4.** Transfer the tenderloins to a carving board and let stand for 3 minutes. Slice on the diagonal into ½-inch-wide pieces. Stir any meat juices on the board into the remaining pomegranate sauce. Serve, with any remaining sauce drizzled over the pork.

One 1½-pound package of pork tenderloins usually contains two 12-ounce tenderloins, not one large one. Always fold back the thin end of each tenderloin and tie it with kitchen string so the meat is evenly thick throughout its length. If you don't, the thin ends will overcook.

# Park's Pork Chops with Pasta Pilaf

### MAKES 4 SERVINGS

Middle Eastern flavors are finding their way into the American kitchen. Even though Muslim cooks would never serve their beloved pasta-and-rice pilaf with pork, it makes a good match for thick chops.

1 TEASPOON GROUND CUMIN

1 TEASPOON DRIED OREGANO

¼ TEASPOON GROUND CINNAMON

1 TEASPOON SALT

3 TABLESPOONS OLIVE OIL

FOUR 8-OUNCE CENTER-CUT PORK CHOPS

4 OUNCES VERMICELLI PASTA, BROKEN INTO 1-INCH
   LENGTHS

1 MEDIUM ONION, CHOPPED

1 GARLIC CLOVE, MINCED

1 CUP LONG-GRAIN RICE

1½ CUPS BEEF BROTH, PREFERABLY HOMEMADE, OR
   USE LOW-SODIUM CANNED BROTH

½ CUP DRY WHITE WINE, SUCH AS CHARDONNAY

1 BAY LEAF

¼ TEASPOON FRESHLY GROUND BLACK PEPPER

2 TABLESPOONS FINELY CHOPPED FRESH PARSLEY

**1.** Position a rack in the center of the oven and pre-heat to 400°F. Lightly oil a 15 × 10-inch baking dish. In a small bowl, mix the cumin, oregano, cinnamon, and ½ teaspoon salt. Season the pork chops with the cumin mixture and set aside.

**2.** In a large (12-inch) nonstick skillet, heat 1 table-spoon oil over high heat. Add the pork chops and cook, turning once, until browned on both sides, about 5 minutes. Transfer to a plate and set aside.

**3.** Add 1 tablespoon oil to the skillet and heat over medium heat. Add the vermicelli and cook, stirring often, until golden brown, about 2 minutes. Remove

and set aside. Add the remaining 1 tablespoon oil to the skillet and heat. Add the onion and garlic and cook until the onion softens, about 3 minutes. Return the vermicelli to the skillet and stir in the rice. Add the broth, wine, ½ cup water, the bay leaf, remaining ½ teaspoon salt, and the pepper. Bring to a boil. Transfer to the prepared baking dish. Place the pork chops on top of the rice mixture and cover tightly with aluminum foil.

**4.** Bake until the rice is tender, about 30 minutes. Discard the bay leaf. Sprinkle the pork chops and rice with the parsley and serve.

# Pork Chops with
# Three Peppers and Olives

### MAKES 4 SERVINGS

A colorful mix of sweet peppers, spiked with olives and orange and seasoned with sage, makes a savory bed for skillet-browned pork chops. I serve these with cooked orzo, tossed with butter and Parmesan cheese.

2 TABLESPOONS OLIVE OIL

FOUR 8-OUNCE CENTER-CUT PORK LOIN CHOPS

½ TEASPOON SALT

½ TEASPOON FRESHLY GROUND BLACK PEPPER

2 MEDIUM RED BELL PEPPERS, SEEDED AND CUT INTO
   ½-INCH-WIDE STRIPS

2 MEDIUM YELLOW BELL PEPPERS, SEEDED AND
   CUT INTO ½-INCH-WIDE STRIPS

1 MEDIUM CUBANELLE OR SMALL GREEN BELL PEPPER,
   SEEDED AND CUT INTO ½-INCH-WIDE STRIPS

2 GARLIC CLOVES, MINCED

GRATED ZEST OF 1 ORANGE

½ CUP FRESH ORANGE JUICE

2 TABLESPOONS BALSAMIC VINEGAR

1 TABLESPOON CHOPPED FRESH SAGE, OR
   1 TEASPOON DRIED

½ CUP BLACK MEDITERRANEAN OLIVES, PITTED

**1.** In a large (12-inch) nonstick skillet, heat 1 tablespoon oil over high heat. Add the pork chops and cook, turning once, until browned on both sides, about 5 minutes. Transfer to a plate and season with ¼ teaspoon each salt and pepper.

**2.** Add the remaining 1 tablespoon oil to the skillet and reduce the heat to medium. Add the red, yellow, and Cubanelle peppers and the garlic. Cook, stirring often, until softened, about 5 minutes. Stir in the zest, juice, vinegar, sage, and remaining ¼ teaspoon each salt and pepper.

**3.** Return the pork chops to the skillet and cover tightly. Reduce heat to medium-low and cook until the pork chops show no sign of pink when pierced at the bone, about 20 minutes. Transfer the chops to a platter and cover with foil to keep warm.

**4.** Add the olives to the skillet and bring to a boil over high heat. Cook, stirring occasionally, until the juices have reduced to a glaze, about 2 minutes. Pour over the chops and serve immediately.

# Adobo-Grilled Pork Chops with Cucumber-Radish Salsa

**MAKES 4 SERVINGS**

The open-air market in Juárez, Mexico, just over the border from El Paso, is a culinary circus, alive with bright colors and mouthwatering food. One of my favorite meals is a spit-roasted, chile-rubbed pork, sliced and served with a spicy vegetable salsa. I've adapted the recipe for pork chops, so there's no hassling with the rotisserie. If you can, marinate the pork chops all day, but if you're in a hurry, a short soak will be fine.

**FOR THE ADOBO**

3 OUNCES MILD DRIED NEW MEXICO CHILES,
    WIPED WITH A DAMP CLOTH
2 TEASPOONS WHOLE CUMIN SEEDS
1 TABLESPOON DRIED OREGANO
2 TABLESPOONS CIDER VINEGAR
1 TEASPOON SUGAR
3 GARLIC CLOVES
¼ TEASPOON SALT
EIGHT 6-OUNCE CENTER-CUT LOIN PORK CHOPS

**FOR THE SALSA**

2 MEDIUM CUCUMBERS, PEELED, SEEDED, AND
    CUT INTO ¼-INCH CUBES
1 CUP GRATED RADISHES (ABOUT 4 OUNCES)
½ CUP MINCED WHITE OR YELLOW ONION
2 TABLESPOONS CHOPPED FRESH CILANTRO
2 TABLESPOONS FRESH LIME JUICE
¼ TEASPOON GROUND MILD CHILE PEPPER,
    SUCH AS CHIMAYO, OR CHILI POWDER
¼ TEASPOON SALT

**1.** To make the adobo, pull off and discard the chile stems. Split the chiles open lengthwise, and discard the seeds and ribs. Place the chiles in a medium bowl and cover with boiling water. Let stand until the chiles soften, about 20 minutes. Drain, reserving the soaking liquid.

**2.** Meanwhile, heat a medium, empty skillet over medium heat. Add the cumin seeds and stir for 30 seconds. Add the oregano and stir until the cumin is toasted, about 30 more seconds. Immediately pour into a blender. Add the drained chiles, 1 cup of the soaking liquid, the vinegar, sugar, garlic, and salt. Blend until pureed, adding more of the soaking liquid if needed to smooth the mixture.

**3.** Pour into a large glass baking dish. Add the pork chops and turn to coat with the adobo. Cover and refrigerate for at least 30 minutes or up to 8 hours.

**4.** To make the salsa, mix the cucumbers, radishes, onion, cilantro, lime juice, ground chile, and salt in a medium bowl. Cover and refrigerate until ready to serve.

**5.** Build a hot charcoal fire in an outdoor grill and let burn until the coals are covered with white ash. Or pre-heat a gas grill on high. Lightly oil the grill. Place the pork chops on the grill and cover. Cook, turning occasionally, until the pork chops feel firm when pressed in the meatiest part, about 10 minutes. Serve immediately with the salsa.

# Honey-Glazed Spareribs

### MAKES 8 SERVINGS

There was this old gentleman with a white mustache who used to say that chicken was finger-lickin' good. Well, while I was taught to respect my elders, I have to disagree. I can't imagine anything that makes me want to lick my digits more than barbecued spareribs rubbed with a bourbon-scented spice paste, then sweetly glazed with honey. You'll really love this method of grilling ribs, where they're precooked over coals to simmer in their own juices before glazing. This trick cooks away the fat, leaving the ribs melt-in-your-mouth tender.

**FOR THE BOURBON SPICE PASTE**

¼ CUP CHILI POWDER

1 TABLESPOON DRIED OREGANO

1 TABLESPOON SWEET HUNGARIAN PAPRIKA

2 TEASPOONS GROUND CUMIN

2 TEASPOONS ONION POWDER

2 TEASPOONS SALT

1 TEASPOON GARLIC POWDER

1 TEASPOON FRESHLY GROUND BLACK PEPPER

⅓ CUP BOURBON

3 TABLESPOONS VEGETABLE OIL

**TO COMPLETE THE RECIPE**

6 POUNDS SPARERIBS, CUT INTO 6 OR 7 RIB SLABS

½ CUP HONEY

⅓ CUP BOURBON

2 TABLESPOONS UNSALTED BUTTER

**1.** To make the bourbon spice paste, mix all of the dry ingredients in a small bowl. Add the bourbon and oil and mix into a paste.

**2.** Spread the paste evenly over the ribs. Double-wrap each slab of ribs with aluminum foil. Let stand at room temperature while building the fire. (Or refrigerate for up to 8 hours, removing from the refrigerator 1 hour before cooking.)

**3.** Build a hot fire in an outdoor grill and let the coals burn until covered with white ash. Or preheat a gas grill on high, then adjust the heat to low. Grill the foil-wrapped ribs, turning occasionally, for 1 hour. The coals will burn down, but that's fine. Transfer the ribs to a large roasting pan and set aside. (The ribs can be prepared up to 1 hour ahead and stored at room temperature, or refrigerated for up to 4 hours.)

**4.** Meanwhile, in a small saucepan over low heat, bring the honey, bourbon, and butter to a simmer. Set aside.

**5.** Add more charcoal to the fire and let it burn until covered with white ash and medium hot—you should be able to hold your hand over the coals for 3 to 4 seconds. Or adjust the heat on a gas grill to medium. Lightly oil the grill. Being careful of the hot juices in the foil, unwrap the ribs. Grill the unwrapped ribs, brushing with the honey glaze and turning occasionally, until browned and lightly glazed, about 10 minutes. Transfer the ribs to a cutting board and let stand for 5 minutes before cutting into individual ribs.

# Ginger-Peachy Ham

Is it an overstatement or an assumption to say that everyone needs a good glazed ham recipe? If you have tired of the standard brown sugar goop, here's a sweet-and-zesty glaze that is interesting, but still something that the whole family will love. Simmering the ham before baking helps to remove excess saltiness.

ONE 8- TO 9-POUND SMOKED HAM WITH SKIN AND BONE

1 CUP PEACH PRESERVES

¼ CUP DIJON MUSTARD

2 TABLESPOONS GRATED FRESH GINGER (USE THE LARGE HOLES ON A BOX GRATER)

2 GARLIC CLOVES, CRUSHED UNDER A KNIFE AND PEELED

**1.** Place the ham in a large stockpot and add cold water to cover. Bring to a boil over medium heat (this could take 30 minutes or so). Reduce the heat to low and simmer for 10 minutes.

**2.** In a blender, combine the peach preserves, mustard, ginger, and garlic and process until smooth. Set aside.

**3.** Preheat the oven to 350°F. Completely line a large roasting pan with aluminum foil. Drain the ham. Using a sharp knife, cut away the rind, leaving a very thin layer of fat on the ham. Score the fat into a diamond pattern. Place the ham on a roasting rack in the pan. Place the pan in the oven and add enough water to come 1 inch up the sides of the pan. Bake the ham, basting occasionally with the water, adding more water to the pan if needed, until a meat thermometer inserted in the thickest part reads 140°F, about 2 hours. Brush a thick layer of the peach mixture over the ham. Continue baking, brushing with the remaining peach mixture about every 10 minutes, until the ham is nicely glazed, about 30 more minutes. Let the ham stand for 10 minutes before carving. Serve hot, warm, or at room temperature.

A large stockpot does the best job for blanching the ham. If you don't have one big enough to do the job, place the ham in an oval turkey roaster, even though the ham won't be covered completely by the water. Turn the ham occasionally so it blanches evenly.

A smoked ham is usually precooked, but tastes much better if baked through before carving. The water in the roasting pan will keep the interior of the oven moist and discourage the ham from drying out. Allow about 15 minutes per pound of ham to bake at 350°F to an internal temperature of 155°F.

If your grill has a rotisserie, use it to cook the blanched ham, brushing it with the glaze during the last 30 minutes.

# Smoked Pork Chops with Autumn Fruits and Applejack

## MAKES 4 SERVINGS

This combination of smoked pork chops, autumn fruits, warm spices, and heady applejack is a supper for a cool evening. Pass the mashed potatoes.

1 TABLESPOON VEGETABLE OIL

FOUR 8-OUNCE SMOKED PORK CHOPS, ON THE BONE

2 TABLESPOONS UNSALTED BUTTER

2 MEDIUM ONIONS, CUT INTO THIN HALF-MOONS

⅛ TEASPOON SALT

¼ TEASPOON FRESHLY GROUND BLACK PEPPER

2 MEDIUM GRANNY SMITH APPLES, PEELED, CORED, AND CUT INTO ½-INCH-THICK WEDGES

2 FIRM-RIPE, MEDIUM BOSC PEARS, PEELED, CORED, AND CUT LENGTHWISE INTO ½-INCH-THICK SLICES

½ TEASPOON DRIED SAGE

½ TEASPOON DRIED ROSEMARY

¼ CUP APPLEJACK OR CALVADOS

½ CUP BEEF BROTH, PREFERABLY HOMEMADE, OR USE LOW-SODIUM CANNED BROTH

**1.** Position a rack in the center of the oven and pre-heat to 375°F. In a large (12-inch) nonstick skillet, heat the oil over medium-high heat. Add the pork chops and cook, turning once, until browned on both sides, about 5 minutes. Set aside.

**2.** Add 1 tablespoon butter to the skillet. Add the onions and cook, stirring often, until golden brown, about 10 minutes. Season with the salt and pepper. Transfer to a 13 × 9-inch baking dish.

**3.** Add the remaining 1 tablespoon butter to the skil-let and heat. Add the apples, pears, sage, and rosemary. Cook, stirring often, until lightly browned, about

3 minutes. Stir into the onions and top with the pork chops. Pour in the broth and applejack. Cover tightly with aluminum foil.

**4.** Bake until the pork chops are heated through and the fruit is tender, about 20 minutes. Serve immedi-ately.

Boneless smoked pork chops are sometimes easier to find than ones on the bone, but they don't have as much flavor (and you don't get to gnaw the bone, either!). If necessary, substitute regular center-cut pork chops.

# Grilled Leg of Lamb with Mediterranean Yogurt Marinade

Butterflied leg of lamb is a perennial grilling favorite, and there is probably a different marinade for every backyard in America. This one is based on yogurt, a tenderizing trick that Mediterranean cooks have used for centuries. The yogurt burns off, leaving a nicely browned crust and tangy flavor—don't think this is going to taste like something you'd put on top of granola. A whole butterflied leg of lamb has a rough surface, making it hard to cook evenly (the thin parts are too well done, and the thick parts are too rare). To solve this problem, I have started cutting the boned lamb into two roasts, and butterflying each, which makes the lamb easier to handle and controls the internal temperature.

**FOR THE MARINADE**

1 MEDIUM ONION, COARSELY CHOPPED

4 GARLIC CLOVES, PEELED

¼ CUP CHOPPED FRESH MINT

2 TABLESPOONS DRIED OREGANO

2 TABLESPOONS TOASTED CUMIN SEEDS
   (SEE OPPOSITE PAGE), GROUND

1 TEASPOON SALT

½ TEASPOON CRUSHED HOT RED PEPPER FLAKES

2 CUPS PLAIN YOGURT

**TO COMPLETE THE RECIPE**

ONE 5½-POUND BONELESS LEG OF LAMB, WELL TRIMMED
   OF FAT, CUT INTO 2 LARGE ROASTS, EACH BUTTERFLIED

**1.** To make the marinade, combine all ingredients but the yogurt in a food processor and process until very finely chopped. Transfer to a large shallow dish (glass is best) and stir in the yogurt.

**2.** Add the boned lamb and turn to coat with the marinade. Cover and refrigerate for at least 4 hours and up to 24 hours. Remove the lamb from the refrigerator 1 hour before grilling.

**3.** Bank charcoal briquettes on one side of a charcoal grill, and let the coals burn until covered with white ash. Lightly oil the grill grid. Cook the lamb directly over the coals, turning once, until seared, about 5 minutes on each side. Transfer to the other side of the grid, not over the coals, and cover with the grill lid. Cook until a meat thermometer inserted in the thickest parts of the meat reads 130°F (for medium-rare meat), about 20 minutes. (For gas grills, cook the lamb over high heat, turning once, to sear for 10 minutes. Reduce the heat to low and continue grilling until cooked to desired doneness, about 20 minutes for medium-rare meat.) Let the lamb stand for about 5 minutes before slicing across the grain.

To toast cumin seeds, heat an empty medium skillet over medium heat. Add the cumin seeds and cook, stirring often, until toasted and fragrant (the seeds may begin to jump out of the pan, so have a lid handy), about 2 minutes. Transfer to a plate and cool.

# Mint Julep Lamb Chops

Bourbon, Dijon mustard, and garlic are three of my favorite cooking ingredients—I'm glad that they go together so well to make this terrific marinade. It works with any kind of lamb chop. I've used shoulder chops, as they are the most common and least expensive, but rib chops or leg of lamb steaks are also good choices.

⅓ CUP BOURBON

2 TABLESPOONS VEGETABLE OIL

1 TABLESPOON DIJON MUSTARD

1 TABLESPOON CHOPPED FRESH MINT

2 TEASPOONS LIGHT BROWN SUGAR

2 GARLIC CLOVES, MINCED

EIGHT 8-OUNCE LAMB SHOULDER CHOPS

**1.** To make the marinade, whisk together the bourbon, oil, mustard, mint, brown sugar, and garlic in a medium bowl until combined. Transfer to a large, self-sealing plastic bag.

**2.** Add the lamb chops and turn to coat in the marinade. Close the bag and refrigerate for at least 1 hour or up to overnight.

**3.** Build a hot charcoal fire in an outdoor grill and let the coals burn until covered with white ash. Or preheat a gas grill on high. Lightly oil the grill. Grill the chops, turning once, 8 to 10 minutes for medium-rare chops. Serve immediately.

# Lamb Shanks in Mole Sauce

Mole, that exotic blend of chiles, nuts, spices, and a dash of chocolate, is a sure way to crank up the flavor volume of braised lamb shanks. The bad news: homemade mole is quite a chore to make. The good news: you can buy very good, ready-made mole in jars at Hispanic markets or by mail order, but get the brown or brick-red, not the green, variety. The recipe makes lots of deliciously spicy sauce, so serve these with warm tortillas to soak up every bit.

2 TABLESPOONS OLIVE OIL, PLUS MORE AS NEEDED

SIX 1-POUND LAMB SHANKS

½ TEASPOON SALT

1 MEDIUM ONION, CHOPPED

2 GARLIC CLOVES, MINCED

2 CUPS BEEF BROTH, PREFERABLY HOMEMADE, OR USE LOW-SODIUM CANNED BROTH

1 CUP HEARTY RED WINE, SUCH AS ZINFANDEL

ONE 8¼-OUNCE JAR BROWN MOLE, WELL STIRRED

WARMED CORN OR FLOUR TORTILLAS, FOR SERVING

**1.** Position a rack in the center of the oven and preheat to 300°F. In a large Dutch oven, heat 1 tablespoon oil over medium-high heat. In batches without crowding, and adding more oil as needed, brown the shanks on all sides, about 10 minutes. Transfer to a large plate, season with salt, and set aside.

**2.** Add the remaining 1 tablespoon oil to the Dutch oven and heat over medium heat. Add the onion and garlic and cook, stirring often, until golden, about 5 minutes. Add the broth, wine, and mole and whisk until smooth. Return the lamb to the Dutch oven and bring to a simmer. Remove from heat.

**3.** Cover tightly and bake until the shanks are very tender, about 1³/4 hours. Halfway through baking, switch the position of the shanks in the Dutch oven from top to bottom so they cook evenly in the sauce. Transfer the shanks to a deep serving platter and cover with foil to keep warm. Off heat, let the sauce stand in the Dutch oven for 5 minutes. Using a large spoon, skim off fat from the surface and pour the sauce over the shanks. Serve hot, with the tortillas.

# Veal and Artichoke Stew with Gremolata

### MAKES 6 SERVINGS

Artichoke hearts are an unexpected surprise in this elegant stew, which gets an added spark from a finish of gremolata, a fragrant blend of parsley and the zest of orange and lemon.

**FOR THE STEW**

3 TABLESPOONS OLIVE OIL

1/3 CUP ALL-PURPOSE FLOUR

1/2 TEASPOON SALT

1/4 TEASPOON FRESHLY GROUND BLACK PEPPER

2 1/2 POUNDS VEAL SHOULDER, CUT INTO 1-INCH CUBES

1 MEDIUM ONION, CHOPPED

2 GARLIC CLOVES, MINCED

4 ANCHOVY FILLETS IN OIL, DRAINED AND
 FINELY CHOPPED

1 TEASPOON DRIED BASIL

1/2 TEASPOON DRIED OREGANO

1 CUP DRY WHITE WINE, SUCH AS CHARDONNAY

ONE 14 1/2-OUNCE CAN TOMATOES IN JUICE,
 DRAINED AND CHOPPED

1 CUP CHICKEN BROTH, PREFERABLY HOMEMADE,
 OR USE LOW-SODIUM CANNED BROTH

1 BAY LEAF

TWO 10-OUNCE PACKAGES THAWED FROZEN ARTICHOKE
 HEARTS

**FOR THE GREMOLATA**

2 TABLESPOONS CHOPPED FRESH PARSLEY

GRATED ZEST OF 1/2 ORANGE

GRATED ZEST OF 1 LEMON

**1.** Position a rack in the center of the oven and preheat to 300°F. In a Dutch oven or flameproof casserole, heat 2 tablespoons oil over medium-high heat. In a shallow dish, mix the flour, salt, and pepper. In batches, toss the veal in the flour, shaking off the excess flour, and add to the Dutch oven. Cook until browned, about 5 minutes. Transfer to a plate and set aside.

**2.** Add the remaining 1 tablespoon oil to the Dutch oven and heat. Add the onion and garlic and cook until the onion softens, about 3 minutes. Add the anchovies, basil, and oregano and stir until the anchovies dissolve, about 1 minute. Add the wine and bring to a boil. Stir in the tomatoes, broth, and bay leaf and bring to a boil.

**3.** Cover tightly and bake until the veal is tender, about 1 1/2 hours. During the last 10 minutes, stir in the artichokes.

4. To make the gremolata, mix the parsley, orange zest, and lemon zest in a small bowl. Just before serving, discard the bay leaf, and sprinkle the stew with the gremolata.

Mediterranean cooks know that anchovies are a great way to season meat dishes. The little fish dissolve into the sauce, leaving an elusive salty flavor that no one will be able to put their finger on. Unless you tell them this stew has anchovies, they'll never know.

# meatless main courses

I'M A DYED-IN-THE-WOOL, CARD-CARRYING CARNIVORE, BUT THE STRANGEST THING HAS been happening lately. More and more, when I sit down to supper, I'm eating like a vegetarian. Without even noticing, I have been cooking an increasing number of meatless main courses, and not missing the meat. When I was growing up (and it wasn't very long ago), if there wasn't meat on the table, it wasn't supper, but now meat is just one of many options.

There are many reasons for this change. We are getting better produce, both at the supermarket and at the many farmer's markets springing up all over the country. People are becoming familiar with ethnic cuisines, and many of these are based on diets that are rich in vegetables, beans, and grains, but low in meat-based proteins. In Chapter Seven, you will find more vegetable-based pasta dishes.

# Grilled Eggplant Parmesan

Old-fashioned eggplant Parmesan sure is good, but the fried eggplant can make it as heavy as a heifer in a pickup. Try my lightened version, with grilled, not fried, eggplant slices.

1 MEDIUM EGGPLANT, SLICED CROSSWISE INTO 12 ROUNDS

2 TEASPOONS SALT

**FOR THE SAUCE**

2 TABLESPOONS EXTRA-VIRGIN OLIVE OIL

1 MEDIUM ONION, MINCED

2 GARLIC CLOVES, MINCED

ONE 28-OUNCE CAN TOMATOES IN JUICE,
    JUICES RESERVED, CHOPPED

⅛ TEASPOON CRUSHED HOT RED PEPPER FLAKES

2 TABLESPOONS FINELY CHOPPED FRESH BASIL

**TO COMPLETE THE RECIPE**

3 TABLESPOONS EXTRA-VIRGIN OLIVE OIL, OR
    MORE AS NEEDED

¼ TEASPOON FRESHLY GROUND BLACK PEPPER

8 OUNCES MOZZARELLA CHEESE, THINLY SLICED,
    TRIMMED TO FIT EGGPLANT

**1.** Place the eggplant slices in a large colander and sprinkle with the salt. Let stand until the eggplant gives off droplets of brown juice, 30 to 60 minutes. Rinse the eggplant well under cold running water, then pat completely dry with paper towels. Set aside.

**2.** Meanwhile, to make the sauce, in a medium saucepan, heat the oil over medium heat. Add the onion and garlic and cook, stirring occasionally, until softened, about 3 minutes. Add the tomatoes with their juices and red pepper flakes; bring to a simmer. Reduce the heat to medium-low and simmer until the juices thicken, about 25 minutes. If desired, puree the sauce in a blender or food processor. Stir in the basil. Set the sauce aside. Reheat before serving.

**3.** Build a hot charcoal fire in an outdoor grill and let burn until covered with white ash. Or preheat a gas grill on high. Lightly oil the grill. Brush both sides of the eggplant with the oil. Grill, covered, until the undersides of the eggplant rounds are golden brown, about 3 minutes. Turn and season with the pepper. Top each slice with cheese. Cover and grill until the eggplant is tender and the cheese is melted, about 3 minutes more.

**4.** To serve, spoon a pool of sauce onto each dinner plate, and top with 2 or 3 eggplant slices. Serve immediately.

Many cooks are in the habit of salting eggplant to release any bitter juices. If the eggplant is very fresh, you can skip this step, but season it just before grilling. Most supermarket eggplant will benefit from presalting.

# Black Bean and Cheese Chilaquiles

MAKES 4 TO 6 SERVINGS

*Chilaquiles* are kind of a quick enchilada pie, originally devised as a way to use up stale tortillas. Most modern kitchens don't have the stale tortilla problem, so it's easier to dry out the tortillas in an oven. Like New Mexican chili, there are red *chilaquiles* made with a dried red chile sauce, and green *chilaquiles* with a tomatillo base. Here's a "green" recipe.

TWELVE 6-INCH CORN TORTILLAS, TORN INTO QUARTERS

**TOMATILLO SAUCE**
1½ POUNDS FRESH TOMATILLOS, HUSKED, OR
    THREE 10-OUNCE CANS, DRAINED AND RINSED
⅓ CUP CHOPPED ONION
¼ CUP COARSELY CHOPPED FRESH CILANTRO
1 JALAPEÑO PEPPER, SEEDED AND COARSELY CHOPPED
2 GARLIC CLOVES, CHOPPED
¾ TEASPOON DRIED OREGANO

¼ TEASPOON SALT
⅛ TEASPOON SUGAR
2 TABLESPOONS VEGETABLE OIL
½ CUP VEGETABLE OR CHICKEN BROTH, PREFERABLY
    HOMEMADE, OR USE LOW-SODIUM CANNED BROTH

**TO COMPLETE THE RECIPE**
ONE 15-OUNCE CAN BLACK BEANS, DRAINED AND RINSED
1 CUP GRATED MONTEREY JACK CHEESE

**1.** Position the oven racks in the center and top third of the oven and preheat to 350°F. Spread the tortillas on baking sheets and spray lightly with the vegetable oil. Bake, stirring occasionally, until they are leathery but not hard, about 10 minutes. Set the tortillas aside to cool. Keep the oven on.

**2.** Meanwhile, make the sauce: Bring a medium saucepan of lightly salted water to a boil over high heat. Add the tomatillos and return to a simmer. Reduce the

heat to medium-low and simmer until the tomatillos are tender but not bursting, 6 to 10 minutes, depending on the size of the tomatillos. (If using canned tomatillos, do not precook.) Drain the tomatillos and transfer to a blender or food processor. Add the onion, cilantro, jalapeño, garlic, oregano, salt, and sugar and puree.

**3.** In a large (12-inch) nonstick ovenproof skillet (if necessary, wrap the handle in aluminum foil to protect it in the oven), heat the oil over medium heat. Add the sauce (it will splatter) and broth and bring to a boil. Reduce the heat to medium-low and simmer until slightly thickened, about 3 minutes.

4. Add half of the tortilla pieces, a few at a time, pushing them under the sauce with a spoon. Scatter the beans and $1/2$ cup of the cheese over the top. Gradually add the remaining tortillas, spooning the sauce over the top until completely covered. Sprinkle with the remaining cheese. Bake until the cheese is melted and the tortillas have absorbed the sauce, about 10 minutes. Serve hot.

# Orzo-Stuffed Peppers with Zinfandel-Tomato Sauce

MAKES 6 SERVINGS

These luscious peppers are about as far away as you can get from the stodgy ground-meat-stuffed ones. Italian-flavored canned stewed tomatoes (already seasoned with vegetables and spices) make a fast sauce. Orzo is a rice-shaped pasta, but if you can't locate it, use small elbow macaroni or ditali (tiny tube-shaped pasta).

6 MEDIUM (6 OUNCES EACH) RED OR YELLOW
    BELL PEPPERS

2 TABLESPOONS OLIVE OIL

¼ TEASPOON SALT, PLUS MORE TO TASTE

½ TEASPOON FRESHLY GROUND BLACK PEPPER

8 OUNCES (1⅓ CUPS) ORZO

1 MEDIUM ONION, CHOPPED

2 GARLIC CLOVES, MINCED

1 CUP FINELY CHOPPED MOZZARELLA CHEESE

¼ CUP FRESHLY GRATED PARMESAN CHEESE

ONE 16-OUNCE CAN ITALIAN-STYLE STEWED TOMATOES

½ CUP ZINFANDEL, OR OTHER DRY, HEARTY RED WINE

¼ TEASPOON DRIED BASIL

**1.** Position a rack in the center of the oven and preheat to 350°F. Lightly oil a baking dish large enough to hold the peppers snugly. Cut the tops off the peppers to form lids. Scoop out the ribs and seeds from each pepper. Rub the peppers and their lids with 1 tablespoon oil. Season the insides of the peppers with the salt and ¼ teaspoon pepper. Set aside.

**2.** Bring a large pot of lightly salted water to a boil over high heat. Add the orzo and cook until almost, but not quite, tender, about 6 minutes. Drain in a wire sieve and rinse under cold running water. Transfer to a medium bowl.

**3.** Meanwhile, in a medium skillet, heat the remaining 1 tablespoon oil over medium heat. Add the onion and garlic and cook, stirring occasionally, until golden, about 5 minutes. Mix into the orzo, along with the mozzarella and Parmesan cheeses and remaining ¼ teaspoon pepper. Season with salt, if desired. Fill the peppers with the orzo stuffing and top with the lids. Place the peppers in the prepared dish.

**4.** In a blender or food processor, pulse the stewed tomatoes, wine, and basil to form a chunky sauce. Pour the sauce over and around the peppers. Cover tightly with foil. Bake until the peppers are heated through, about 1 hour. Serve hot.

# Roast Vegetable and Provolone Pizza

Now that every supermarket carries packaged, prebaked pizza crusts, ready to be topped at will, homemade pizza can be prepared with very little effort. Roasted vegetables combined with sharp provolone cheese make a meatless version out of the ordinary.

1 MEDIUM ZUCCHINI, SLICED LENGTHWISE INTO
   ½-INCH-WIDE STRIPS

1 LARGE PORTOBELLO MUSHROOM, STEM REMOVED,
   CAP AND STEM SLICED INTO ½-INCH-WIDE STRIPS

1 SMALL RED BELL PEPPER, SEEDED AND CUT INTO
   ½-INCH-WIDE STRIPS

1 RED ONION, SLICED INTO ¼-INCH-THICK HALF-MOONS

2 TABLESPOONS OLIVE OIL

¼ TEASPOON SALT

¼ TEASPOON FRESHLY GROUND BLACK PEPPER

2 GARLIC CLOVES, MINCED

ONE 16-OUNCE PACKAGE PREBAKED PIZZA CRUST,
   SUCH AS BOBOLI

1⅓ CUPS (5 OUNCES) GRATED SHARP PROVOLONE CHEESE

½ TEASPOON DRIED BASIL

½ TEASPOON DRIED OREGANO

¼ TEASPOON CRUSHED HOT RED PEPPER FLAKES

**1.** Position a rack in the top third of the oven and preheat to 450°F. Place the zucchini, mushroom cap and stem, red pepper, and onion on a large baking sheet and toss with the oil, salt, and pepper. Roast, stirring occasionally, until the vegetables are tender, about 20 minutes. Stir the garlic into the vegetables and set aside. Keep the oven at 450°F.

**2.** Place the pizza crust on a large baking sheet. Sprinkle with the cheese. Arrange the vegetables over the crust. Bake until the crust heats through and cheese melts, about 10 minutes. Sprinkle with the basil, oregano, and red pepper flakes. Serve immediately.

# Corn and Tomato Risotto

MAKES 6 SERVINGS

Risotto, with its smooth, creamy texture, has become one of the top comfort foods of the nineties. Imported Italian rice, starchier than other varieties, is the only rice that makes a proper, creamy risotto. Don't believe those who say that you have to stand over the risotto and stir it constantly. If you have a good, heavy Dutch oven (such as Le Creuset), you can leave the simmering pot for a couple of minutes to set the table, rinse the lettuce, or do other supper chores. Here's a recipe that is best during summer's last hurrah.

¼ CUP (½ STICK) UNSALTED BUTTER

1 CUP CHOPPED SCALLIONS, WHITE AND GREEN PARTS

3 CUPS FRESH OR THAWED FROZEN CORN KERNELS

1 LARGE RIPE BEEFSTEAK TOMATO,
SEEDED AND CHOPPED

8 CUPS CHICKEN BROTH, APPROXIMATELY, PREFERABLY
HOMEMADE, OR USE LOW-SODIUM CANNED BROTH

1 POUND IMPORTED ITALIAN RICE FOR RISOTTO,
SUCH AS ARBORIO, VIALONE NANO, OR CARNAROLI

½ CUP DRY WHITE WINE, SUCH AS CHARDONNAY

½ CUP FRESHLY GRATED PARMESAN CHEESE

3 TABLESPOONS CHOPPED FRESH BASIL

½ TEASPOON SALT

¼ TEASPOON FRESHLY GROUND BLACK PEPPER

**1.** In a large, heavy-bottomed Dutch oven or saucepan, melt 2 tablespoons butter over medium heat. Add the scallions and cook until softened, about 2 minutes. Add the corn and cook until heated through, about 5 minutes. Stir in the tomato and cook for 2 minutes. Transfer to a bowl and cover with foil to keep warm.

**2.** In a medium saucepan, bring the sauce to a simmer over high heat. Reduce the heat to very low and keep at a mere simmer.

**3.** Melt the remaining 2 tablespoons butter in the saucepan. Add the rice and cook, stirring almost constantly, until the rice turns evenly opaque, about 2 minutes. Pour in the wine. Cook, stirring often, until the rice absorbs the wine, about 2 minutes. Ladle in about 1 cup of the hot broth. Stir often until the rice absorbs the broth, 2 to 3 minutes. Continue adding the broth, 1 cup at a time, until the rice is al dente, tender with a slight firmness in the center. The entire process will take about 25 minutes. During the last minute or two, stir in the corn and tomato mixture. When the rice is al dente, stir in 1 cup of broth to give the risotto a spoonable, creamy consistency. Be flexible with your timing and the amount of broth. There may be some broth left over, or if you run out of broth, just use hot water. The important thing is the creamy texture.

**4.** Remove from the heat and stir in the reserved corn and tomato mixture, the cheese, basil, salt, and pepper. Serve immediately in warmed soup bowls.

**Risotto Patties:** For every cup of leftover risotto, stir in 1 large egg yolk. Form into 2-inch patties and roll in fresh bread crumbs. Sauté in butter until golden brown on both sides, about 5 minutes.

Good broth will make or break risotto. It doesn't *have* to be homemade—although it would be a good opportunity to thaw that homemade chicken stock that most food writers want you to have in your freezer. If you use a canned broth, use the low-sodium variety, as it tastes better—and don't even think about using bouillon cubes!

Once you get the hang of making risotto (sauté vegetables and set aside, then make the risotto and stir in the vegetables at the end of the cooking time to reheat), you can let inspiration cut loose. Try it with mushrooms, zucchini, sweet red peppers, or sugar snap peas.

# Mozzarella Quesadillas with Tomato Olivada

### MAKES 6 QUESADILLAS, 8 TO 12 SERVINGS

This "new wave" quesadilla adds a little Italian style to the old Tex-Mex reliable. Instead of *queso blanco*, I've used mozzarella, which pizza lovers know melts beautifully, and created an olive-and-caper tomato "salsa" that brings to mind the zesty Italian condiment, *olivada*. Grill the quesadillas to order as you need them, so they don't wait around and get cold.

**FOR THE TOMATO *OLIVADA***

12 OUNCES BLACK MEDITERRANEAN OLIVES, SUCH
   AS KALAMATA, PITTED AND COARSELY CHOPPED
   (1 SCANT CUP)

1 LARGE RIPE BEEFSTEAK TOMATO, SEEDED AND
   CUT INTO ¼-INCH CUBES

1 LARGE ROASTED RED BELL PEPPER, PEELED, SEEDED,
   AND CUT INTO ¼-INCH DICE (SEE OPPOSITE PAGE)

2 TABLESPOONS IMPORTED CAPERS, RINSED,
   CHOPPED IF LARGE

1 TABLESPOON CHOPPED FRESH BASIL

1 TABLESPOON CHOPPED FRESH OREGANO
   (OR MORE BASIL)

1 TABLESPOON RED WINE VINEGAR

1 TABLESPOON EXTRA-VIRGIN OLIVE OIL

1 TEASPOON ANCHOVY PASTE, OR 2 ANCHOVY FILLETS,
   MINCED AND MASHED TO A PASTE

1 GARLIC CLOVE, MINCED AND MASHED TO A PASTE
   WITH A SPRINKLE OF SALT

¼ TEASPOON CRUSHED HOT RED PEPPER FLAKES, OR
   TO TASTE

**TO COMPLETE THE RECIPE**

TWELVE 8-INCH FLOUR TORTILLAS

1½ CUPS (6 OUNCES) GRATED MOZZARELLA CHEESE

**1.** To make the tomato *olivada:* In a medium bowl, mix the olives, tomato, bell pepper, capers, basil, and oregano. In a small bowl, whisk the vinegar, oil, anchovy paste, garlic, and hot pepper flakes to dissolve the anchovy paste. Add to the chopped mixture and mix well. Cover and let stand until ready to serve, preferably for at least 30 minutes.

**2.** Build a charcoal fire in an outdoor grill and let the coals burn until covered with white ash and medium-hot. You should be able to hold your hand over them for about 3 seconds. For each quesadilla, place 1 tortilla on a work surface, sprinkle with ½ cup cheese, and top with another tortilla.

**3.** Place 2 or 3 quesadillas on the grill. Grill until the undersides are lightly toasted, 1 to 1¹/₂ minutes. Carefully flip the quesadillas and toast the other sides. Transfer to a cutting board and cut each quesadilla into 6 to 8 wedges with a sharp knife. Arrange the quesadillas on a serving platter, and serve with a bowl of the *olivada*, allowing guests to spoon a dab of *olivada* onto their quesadillas.

**Variation:**

The quesadilla can also be made indoors, prepared in a skillet. Heat a dry skillet over medium heat. Place 1 tortilla in the skillet and sprinkle with ¹/₄ cup cheese. Top with another tortilla. Cook until the underside is spotted brown, about 1 minute. Turn and cook until the other side is spotted, about 1 minute more. Keep the quesadillas warm in a preheated 200°F oven.

To roast red bell or poblano peppers, position a broiler rack about 6 inches from the source of the heat and preheat the broiler. Broil the peppers, turning occasionally, until blackened and blistered all over, 8 to 12 minutes. Transfer the peppers to a paper bag, close the bag, and let stand for 20 minutes to cool and soften the peppers. Use a small sharp knife to remove the blackened skins.

# Vegetable and Poblano Stew

MAKES 6 TO 8 SERVINGS

I first shared this recipe in my book *Chiles*, but it is such a fine stew, it bears repeating here. It is packed with vegetables and makes an excellent pasta sauce, tossed with penne and Parmesan cheese, and drizzled with extra-virgin olive oil.

1 LARGE EGGPLANT, TRIMMED, QUARTERED, AND CUT INTO ¾-INCH SLICES

4 TEASPOONS SALT, PLUS MORE TO TASTE

1 POUND ORANGE-COLORED WINTER SQUASH, SUCH AS BUTTERNUT, PARED AND CUT INTO ¾-INCH CUBES

½ CUP OLIVE OIL, AS NEEDED

4 POBLANO PEPPERS, ROASTED, SEEDED, AND CUT INTO JULIENNE STRIPS (SEE PAGE 123)

1 MEDIUM ONION, SLICED

4 GARLIC CLOVES, MINCED

2 CUPS FRESH CORN KERNELS AND JUICES, CUT AND SCRAPED FROM 4 MEDIUM EARS, OR 2 CUPS THAWED FROZEN CORN KERNELS

1 CUP CHICKEN BROTH, PREFERABLY HOMEMADE, OR USE LOW-SODIUM CANNED BROTH

½ CUP JULIENNED BASIL LEAVES

**1.** Place the eggplant slices in a large colander and sprinkle with 2 teaspoons salt. Let stand until the eggplant gives off droplets of brown juice, 30 to 60 minutes. Rinse the eggplant well under cold running water, then pat completely dry with paper towels. (If the eggplant is very fresh, you can skip this step.) Set aside.

**2.** Bring a medium saucepan of water to a boil over high heat. Add the squash cubes and the remaining 2 teaspoons salt. Cook, stirring once, until barely tender, about 15 minutes. Drain and set aside.

**3.** In a large (12-inch) nonstick skillet, heat 2 tablespoons of the oil over medium heat. In batches, and adding more oil as needed, cook the eggplant, turning once, until browned on both sides, about 6 minutes. Transfer to a bowl.

**4.** Add 2 tablespoons oil to the skillet and heat over medium heat. Add the poblano peppers, onion, and garlic. Cover and cook, stirring occasionally, until softened, about 10 minutes. Add the eggplant, squash, the corn and juices, and broth and bring to a simmer. Reduce the heat to low and simmer until thick, about 10 minutes. Stir in the basil, cover, and let stand for 1 minute. Season with salt to taste. Serve hot or at room temperature.

# Mushroom-Chile Tamale Pie

MAKES 4 TO 6 SERVINGS

Old-fashioned tamale pie (you know, the kind with hamburger) was a favorite supper dish for many families when I was growing up. I just love breaking into the golden cornmeal crust to find a luscious filling underneath. Nowadays I make a vegetarian version that is just as hearty and satisfying as the ground beef classic.

2 TABLESPOONS OLIVE OIL

1 LARGE ONION, CHOPPED

1 MEDIUM ZUCCHINI, CHOPPED INTO ½-INCH CUBES

1 POUND CREMINI OR BUTTON MUSHROOMS, THINLY
    SLICED

2 GARLIC CLOVES, MINCED

2 TABLESPOONS CHILI POWDER

2 TEASPOONS DRIED OREGANO

1 TEASPOON SALT

ONE 14½-OUNCE CAN TOMATOES IN JUICE, JUICES
    RESERVED, CHOPPED

1 TABLESPOON UNSALTED BUTTER

1 JALAPEÑO PEPPER, SEEDED AND MINCED

2 CUPS COLD WATER

1 CUP YELLOW STONE-GROUND CORNMEAL

1 CUP GRATED SHARP CHEDDAR CHEESE

**1.** Position a rack in the center of the oven and preheat to 350°F. Lightly oil a 10-inch deep-dish pie plate.

**2.** In a large (12-inch) nonstick skillet, heat the oil over medium heat. Add the onion and zucchini and cook until softened, about 5 minutes. Add the mushrooms and garlic. Cook, stirring often, until the mushrooms give off their liquid and it evaporates, about 8 minutes. Add the chili powder, oregano, and ½ teaspoon salt and stir for 30 seconds. Add the tomatoes and their juices and bring to a boil over high heat. Cook until the tomato juices evaporate and the mixture

thickens, about 5 minutes. Transfer to the prepared pie plate.

**3.** Meanwhile, in a medium saucepan, heat the butter over medium heat. Add the jalapeño and cook until softened, about 1 minute. Add 1 cup of the water and the remaining ½ teaspoon salt and bring to a boil over high heat. In a small bowl, whisk the remaining 1 cup water with the cornmeal until smooth. Whisk into the boiling water and bring to a boil. Reduce the heat to medium-low. Cook, whisking constantly, until slightly thickened, about 2 minutes. Whisk in ½ cup of the cheese.

*continued*

**4.** Spread the hot cornmeal over the vegetable mixture. Sprinkle with the remaining ¹/₂ cup cheese. Place on a baking sheet. Bake until the cheese is melted and the filling is bubbling, about 30 minutes. Serve hot.

Stone-ground cornmeal has much more flavor than the mass-processed version. Look for it in bags at supermarkets, or at natural food stores.

# Zucchini and Rice Casserole

If you were to be served this kind of vegetable, rice, and egg casserole in France, *maman* would call it a *tian*. Here, Mom calls it a casserole. Regardless of the name and location, it's a fine example of simple supper fare, and could become a favorite *chez toi*—I mean at your house. It is mouthwatering hot out of the oven, but just as good at room temperature. This casserole is good hot, warm, or at room temperature, but don't serve it cold from the refrigerator. Cold rice firms up into hard pellets and isn't too fun to eat.

½ CUP LONG-GRAIN RICE

3 TABLESPOONS OLIVE OIL

4 MEDIUM (2¼ POUNDS TOTAL) ZUCCHINI, TRIMMED
   AND CUT INTO ⅛-INCH-THICK ROUNDS

2 MEDIUM ONIONS, CHOPPED

1 JALAPEÑO PEPPER, SEEDED AND MINCED

2 GARLIC CLOVES, MINCED

3 LARGE EGGS

3 TABLESPOONS CHOPPED FRESH CILANTRO

½ TEASPOON SALT

¼ TEASPOON FRESHLY GROUND BLACK PEPPER

¾ CUP (3 OUNCES) GRATED SHARP CHEDDAR CHEESE

½ CUP FRESHLY GRATED PARMESAN CHEESE

**1.** Position a rack in the center of the oven and preheat to 350°F. Lightly oil an 11 × 7-inch baking dish.

**2.** Bring a medium saucepan of lightly salted water to a boil over high heat. Add the rice and cook until barely tender, about 15 minutes. Drain in a wire sieve and rinse under cold running water. Set aside.

**3.** Meanwhile, in a large (12-inch) nonstick skillet, heat the oil over medium-high heat. Add the zucchini and cook, turning occasionally, until softened, about 8 minutes. Add the onions, jalapeño, and garlic and cook until softened, about 5 minutes more. Set the zucchini mixture aside.

**4.** In a medium bowl, whisk together the eggs, cilantro, salt, and pepper. Stir in the rice, ¼ cup each cheddar and Parmesan cheeses, then the zucchini mixture. Spread evenly in the prepared dish, and sprinkle with the remaining ½ cup cheddar and ¼ cup Parmesan cheese.

**5.** Bake until the cheese is melted and the casserole looks set in the center, about 30 minutes. Cool for 5 minutes before serving. Serve hot, warm, or at room temperature.

# pasta main courses

IT WAS SOPHIA LOREN WHO ONCE SAID, "ALL YOU SEE HERE I OWE TO PASTA." WHILE PASTA is still the national food of Italy, considering the amount of pasta served here in the last ten years, our national foods (certainly hot dogs and burgers) must be getting nervous.

Fresh pasta is wonderful, but Italian cooks save it for special occasions and holidays, and cook dried pasta for everyday meals. At my house, even though I can get fresh pasta at the supermarket, I always cook with dried pasta.

Here are a few things to remember when cooking pasta.

Cook pasta in plenty of boiling water—at least 4 quarts for a pound of pasta.

Don't leave out the salt, as unsalted pasta tastes flat and dull. Add enough salt to make the water taste a little salty. If you insist on measuring the salt, allow 2 teaspoons for 4 to 5 quarts of water.

There is no need to put any oil in the water, which is supposed to keep the pasta from sticking to itself, but only slicks the pasta and keeps the sauce from clinging properly. Just stir the pasta a few times during the first two minutes of boiling, and it won't stick.

Cook the pasta just until al dente—that is, until it is just tender with a little bit of resistance in the center. If the pasta is going to be cooked further in a gratin, cook it *very* al dente, so it isn't overcooked by the time it is taken out of the oven.

Drain the pasta well, giving tubular-shaped pasta an extra shake to get the water out of the holes. Never rinse pasta, unless it is to be used in a pasta salad. Rinsing removes the surface starch, which is needed to help the sauce coat the pasta well.

# Penne with Broccoli and Blue Cheese

Here's a pasta to make when time is short. Use any kind of blue cheese you like, but if you can get your hands on Maytag Blue from Iowa, you're in for a real treat—an American cheese that can be put on a pedestal with Europe's best.

1 BUNCH BROCCOLI (ABOUT 1¾ POUNDS)

2 TABLESPOONS UNSALTED BUTTER

2 GARLIC CLOVES, MINCED

1 POUND BOW-TIE PASTA

1 CUP RICOTTA CHEESE

4 OUNCES BLUE CHEESE, PREFERABLY MAYTAG BLUE, CRUMBLED, AT ROOM TEMPERATURE

¼ TEASPOON SALT

¼ TEASPOON FRESHLY GROUND BLACK PEPPER

**1.** Using a sharp knife, cut the broccoli florets from the stems. Trim the thick peel from the stalks, and cut the stalks crosswise into ¼-inch-thick rounds. Set the broccoli florets and stems aside.

**2.** In a small skillet, heat the butter over medium-low heat. Add the garlic and cook, stirring often, until just golden, about 2 minutes. Set aside.

**3.** Bring a large pot of lightly salted water to a boil over high heat. Add the stems and cook for 2 minutes. Add the florets and cook until the broccoli is barely tender, about 2 more minutes. Using a large skimmer, transfer the broccoli to a large bowl (no need to rinse) and set aside.

**4.** Add the pasta to the boiling water and cook until tender. Scoop out and reserve ½ cup of the pasta cooking water. Drain the pasta well and return to the warm pot. Add the ricotta, blue cheese, and reserved garlic and butter. Toss, adding enough of the pasta water to make a creamy sauce. Season with the salt and pepper. Serve immediately.

# Macaroni with Chile con Queso

*Chile con queso,* that fabulous, cheesey, creamy dip that I would pour on my cereal in the morning if they'd let me, is a natural for mixing with macaroni to make the hippest macaroni and cheese on either side of the border.

3 TABLESPOONS UNSALTED BUTTER

1 SMALL ONION, CHOPPED

1 MEDIUM CUBANELLE OR SMALL GREEN BELL PEPPER, SEEDED AND CHOPPED

2 GARLIC CLOVES, MINCED

ONE 14½-OUNCE CAN TOMATOES IN JUICE, DRAINED, AND CHOPPED

2 TABLESPOONS ALL-PURPOSE FLOUR

2 CUPS MILK, HEATED

1 CUP (4 OUNCES) GRATED EXTRA-SHARP CHEDDAR CHEESE

1 CUP (4 OUNCES) GRATED JALAPEÑO JACK CHEESE

1 POUND ELBOW MACARONI, COARSELY CRACKED

¾ CUP FRESH BREAD CRUMBS (SEE PAGE 55)

**1.** Position a rack in the center of the oven and preheat to 350°F. Lightly butter a deep 3-quart casserole.

**2.** In a medium saucepan, heat 2 tablespoons of the butter over medium heat. Add the onion, pepper, and garlic. Cook, stirring occasionally, until softened, about 5 minutes. Add the tomatoes and cook until their juices evaporate and the mixture looks somewhat dry, about 5 minutes. Sprinkle with the flour and stir for 1 minute.

**3.** Stir in the milk, bring to a simmer, and cook over medium-low heat, stirring often, until thickened and smooth, about 2 minutes. Remove from the heat and stir in the cheeses until melted.

**4.** Meanwhile, bring a large pot of lightly salted water to a boil over high heat. Add the macaroni and cook until almost tender, about 8 minutes. (The pasta will be cooked again in the oven.) Drain well and return to the cooking pot. Add the cheese sauce and mix well. Transfer to the prepared dish. Sprinkle with the bread crumbs and dot with the remaining 1 tablespoon butter, cut into small pieces.

**5.** Bake until the crumbs are browned and the sauce is bubbling, about 30 minutes. Serve hot.

Jalapeño jack cheese varies in spiciness from brand to brand. Taste a bit first, and if you think your sauce could use more heat, add a seeded and minced jalapeño pepper to the saucepan when cooking the onion mixture.

# Cheese Ravioli in Vegetable-Garlic Broth

MAKES 4 TO 6 SERVINGS

There are many good ravioli brands in the freezer case, and they make a quick, easy, comforting supper. (Look for locally produced brands without any preservatives—the ingredients list should read like they took Grandma's recipe and mass-produced it.) Be sure to cook the ravioli in a separate pot of boiling water, not the broth, as the broth will get cloudy from the pasta. If you wish, you can add a sprinkle of chopped fresh basil or oregano to each serving, but I kind of like the pure flavor of lots of unadorned vegetables with the ravioli.

2 TABLESPOONS EXTRA-VIRGIN OLIVE OIL

1 LARGE ONION, CHOPPED

2 MEDIUM CARROTS, CUT INTO ½-INCH DICE

2 MEDIUM CELERY RIBS, CUT INTO ½-INCH DICE

1 MEDIUM ZUCCHINI, CUT INTO ½-INCH DICE

8 GARLIC CLOVES, CRUSHED UNDER A KNIFE

3 CUPS CHICKEN BROTH, PREFERABLY HOMEMADE, OR USE LOW-SODIUM CANNED BROTH

SALT AND FRESHLY GROUND BLACK PEPPER

TWO 13-OUNCE BAGS FROZEN CHEESE RAVIOLI

FRESHLY GRATED PARMESAN CHEESE, FOR SERVING

**1.** In a medium saucepan, heat the oil over medium heat. Add the onion, carrots, celery, zucchini, and garlic and cover. Cook, stirring occasionally, until the vegetables are tender, about 10 minutes.

**2.** Add the broth and bring to a boil over high heat. Reduce the heat to low and partially cover. Simmer until the flavors are blended, about 15 minutes. Season to taste with salt and pepper.

**3.** Meanwhile, bring a large pot of lightly salted water to a boil. Add the ravioli and reduce the heat to medium. Cook the ravioli at a gentle boil until tender, about 15 minutes. Drain.

**4.** Divide the ravioli among warmed soup bowls and ladle in the vegetables and broth. Serve immediately, with a bowl of the cheese passed on the side for sprinkling.

# Pasta Gratin with Mushrooms and Fontina Cheese

MAKES 4 TO 6 SERVINGS

While this is a macaroni and cheese for grownups, kids that like mushrooms will also go for this sophisticated dish. Choose meaty-textured, full-flavored mushrooms for the gratin. Oyster mushrooms and enoki mushrooms, even though they look great, are too delicate for this dish. *Real* fontina cheese (from northern Italy) is one of the world's great cheeses and worth searching out, but use the Scandinavian version if you can't find it.

1 OUNCE DRIED PORCINI OR POLISH BLACK MUSHROOMS

2 TABLESPOONS UNSALTED BUTTER

1 POUND ASSORTED MUSHROOMS (BUTTON, PORTOBELLO, SHIITAKE, AND CREMINI, IN ANY COMBINATION), TRIMMED AND SLICED

2 GARLIC CLOVES, MINCED

½ TEASPOON SALT

¼ TEASPOON FRESHLY GROUND BLACK PEPPER

1 POUND PENNE, OR OTHER TUBULAR-SHAPED PASTA, SUCH AS ZITI

2 CUPS (8 OUNCES) GRATED FONTINA CHEESE, PREFERABLY ITALIAN

1 CUP RICOTTA CHEESE

1 CUP HEAVY CREAM

¼ CUP FRESHLY GRATED PARMESAN CHEESE

**1.** Position a rack in the top third of the oven and preheat to 450°F. Lightly butter a 15 × 10-inch baking dish.

**2.** In a small bowl, cover the dried mushrooms with 1 cup of boiling water. Let stand until softened, about 20 minutes. (Or place the porcini and 1 cup hot tap water in a small glass bowl and microwave on high for 2 minutes, and let stand for 5 minutes.) Lift the mushrooms out of the soaking liquid (leaving any grit behind in the bottom of the bowl) and coarsely chop; set aside. Strain the soaking liquid through a wire sieve lined with a moistened paper towel and reserve.

**3.** In a large (12-inch) nonstick skillet, heat 1 tablespoon of the butter over medium heat. Add the fresh mushrooms and cook, stirring occasionally, until they begin to give off their juices, about 5 minutes. Add the soaked mushrooms and their strained liquid. Bring to a boil over high heat and cook until the liquid evaporates, about 5 minutes. Stir in the garlic and cook until fragrant, about 30 seconds. Season with the salt and pepper and set aside.

**4.** Meanwhile, bring a large pot of lightly salted water to a boil over high heat. Stir in the penne. Cook, stirring occasionally, until almost, but not quite tender, about 8 minutes. (The pasta will be cooked further in the oven.) Drain, shaking the colander well to remove any excess water from the penne. Return the penne to the pot. Add the mushrooms, fontina, ricotta, and cream and mix.

**5.** Transfer to the prepared dish. Sprinkle with the Parmesan cheese and dot with the remaining 1 tablespoon butter. Bake until the top is crusty brown, about 10 minutes.

# Penne, Lasagne-Style

MAKES 4 TO 6 SERVINGS

Boy, do I love lasagne! But I have to be in the mood for constructing the layers—not that I use a carpenter's level or anything, but it does take a little work. This quick version gives me all of the flavor with half the trouble, mixing penne with a sausage-tomato sauce and cheeses, then giving it a quick bake. Sounds good to me! (And it is!)

1 TABLESPOON OLIVE OIL

1 POUND SWEET ITALIAN PORK OR TURKEY SAUSAGE, CASINGS REMOVED

1 MEDIUM ONION, CHOPPED

2 GARLIC CLOVES, MINCED

1 CUP HEARTY RED WINE, SUCH AS ZINFANDEL

ONE 28-OUNCE CAN TOMATOES WITH TOMATO PUREE, CHOPPED

ONE 6-OUNCE CAN TOMATO PASTE

2 TEASPOONS DRIED BASIL

2 TEASPOONS DRIED OREGANO

¼ TEASPOON CRUSHED HOT RED PEPPER FLAKES

1 POUND PENNE, OR OTHER TUBULAR-SHAPED PASTA, SUCH AS MOSTACOLLI OR ZITI

2 CUPS (8 OUNCES) GRATED MOZZARELLA CHEESE

ONE 15-OUNCE CONTAINER RICOTTA CHEESE

**1.** Preheat the oven to 450°F. Lightly oil a 15 × 10-inch baking dish.

**2.** In a Dutch oven or flameproof casserole, heat the oil over medium heat. Add the sausage, onion, and garlic. Cook, breaking up the sausage with a spoon as it cooks, until the sausage is seared, about 5 minutes. Drain off any fat from the Dutch oven. Add the red wine and bring to a boil. Stir in the tomatoes with their puree, tomato paste, basil, oregano, and red pepper flakes, and break up the tomatoes with the side of a spoon. Bring to a boil, then reduce the heat to medium-low. Simmer, stirring often, until slightly thickened, 20 to 25 minutes.

**3.** Meanwhile, bring a large pot of lightly salted water to a boil over high heat. Stir in the penne. Cook, stirring occasionally, until almost, but not quite, tender, about 8 minutes. Drain, shaking the colander well to remove any excess water from the penne. Stir the penne into the tomato sauce. Stir in the mozzarella and ricotta cheeses.

**4.** Transfer to the prepared baking dish. Bake until the cheese melts and the ends of the penne are crusty brown, about 10 minutes. Serve hot.

Use solid, full-bodied red wines for cooking, such as zinfandel or cabernet sauvignon. These just happen to be great wines to drink with this pasta, too, but choose a reasonably priced, everyday brand. Most pinot noirs and Beaujolais are too light-bodied to stand up to the tomatoes and herbs.

# Going-to-Hell-in-a-Handbasket Pasta

MAKES 4 TO 6 SERVINGS

One look at the devil-may-care list of ingredients, and you'll know how this recipe got its name. Now, I am not saying you should eat this every night. But I am telling you that when you want to make a supper that will have your friends and family literally begging for seconds, make this. Just lie through your teeth, and tell them it's made with skim milk.

1 TABLESPOON OLIVE OIL

1 POUND SWEET ITALIAN PORK OR TURKEY SAUSAGE,
   CASINGS REMOVED

2 GARLIC CLOVES, MINCED

2 CUPS HEAVY CREAM

1 POUND PENNE, OR OTHER TUBULAR-SHAPED PASTA

1 CUP FRESHLY GRATED PARMESAN CHEESE,
   PLUS MORE FOR SERVING

2 TABLESPOONS CHOPPED FRESH PARSLEY

¼ TEASPOON SALT

½ TEASPOON FRESHLY GROUND BLACK PEPPER

**1.** In a large skillet, heat the oil over medium heat. Add the sausage and cook, breaking it up with the side of a large spoon, until browned, about 8 minutes. Pour off the fat from the skillet. Add the garlic to the sausage and cook until softened, about 2 minutes. Add the cream and bring to a boil. Cook, stirring often, until slightly thickened, about 5 minutes. (The sauce can be made 1 hour ahead and kept at room temperature. Reheat to simmering before proceeding.)

**2.** Meanwhile, bring a large pot of lightly salted water to a boil over high heat. Add the pasta and cook until al dente, about 9 minutes. Drain well, shaking the colander well to remove excess water. Return the pasta to the warm cooking pot.

**3.** Add the sauce, cheese, and parsley and mix well. Cover and let stand for 1 minute for the pasta to absorb the sauce. Season with the salt and pepper. Serve immediately, with extra cheese passed on the side.

# Fettuccine with Shrimp Bolognese

Bolognese sauce, typically made with meat and cream, is one fine way to serve fettuccine. Lately, some of those New American Cuisine chef guys (like Todd English at Cambridge's Olive Restaurant and Alfred Portale at Gotham Bar and Grill in Manhattan) have been serving shellfish versions at their restaurants. I came up with my own simple supper recipe, which doesn't call for a battalion of sous-chefs to make well.

2 TABLESPOONS UNSALTED BUTTER

⅓ CUP MINCED SHALLOTS

1 SMALL CARROT, FINELY CHOPPED

1 SMALL CELERY RIB, FINELY CHOPPED

1 GARLIC CLOVE, MINCED

½ CUP DRY WHITE WINE, SUCH AS CHARDONNAY

ONE 14½-OUNCE CAN TOMATOES IN JUICE,
    DRAINED AND CHOPPED

1 CUP BOTTLED CLAM JUICE

⅔ CUP HEAVY CREAM

2 TEASPOONS CHOPPED FRESH TARRAGON, OR
    1 TEASPOON DRIED

1 BAY LEAF

1 POUND MEDIUM SHRIMP, PEELED AND DEVEINED

¼ TEASPOON SALT

¼ TEASPOON FRESHLY GROUND BLACK PEPPER

1 POUND DRIED FETTUCCINE

**1.** In a medium saucepan, heat the butter over medium-low heat. Add the shallots, carrot, celery, and garlic and cover. Cook, stirring occasionally, until the vegetables soften, about 6 minutes. Increase the heat to medium. Add the wine and bring to a boil. Add the tomatoes, clam juice, cream, tarragon, and bay leaf and return to a boil. Reduce the heat to medium-low and simmer until thick enough to lightly coat a wooden spoon, about 20 minutes. Discard the bay leaf.

**2.** Stir in the shrimp and cook until the shrimp are pink and firm, about 3 minutes. Season with the salt and pepper. Set the sauce aside.

**3.** Meanwhile, bring a large pot of lightly salted water to a boil over high heat. Add the fettuccine and cook until barely tender, about 9 minutes. Drain and return to the cooking pot, off heat. Add the sauce and mix well. Cover and let stand for 1 minute to allow the pasta to absorb some of the sauce. Serve immediately.

# Cold Noodles with Chicken and Spicy Peanut Sauce

It was already eight o'clock, steaming hot outside, and we hadn't had dinner yet. A quick look in the refrigerator and pantry, and this is what I came up with—and dinner was served in 15 minutes. If you don't have any leftover chicken as I did, see the following recipe for poached chicken breasts.

½ CUP SMOOTH PEANUT BUTTER, PREFERABLY UNSALTED

½ CUP CHICKEN BROTH, PREFERABLY HOMEMADE, OR
    USE LOW-SODIUM CANNED BROTH

3 TABLESPOONS SOY SAUCE

2 TEASPOONS FRESHLY SQUEEZED GINGER JUICE
    (SEE PAGE 9)

2 GARLIC CLOVES, CRUSHED THROUGH A PRESS

¼ TEASPOON CRUSHED HOT RED PEPPER FLAKES

1 POUND DRIED LINGUINE

3 SCALLIONS, WHITE AND GREEN PARTS, CHOPPED

2 TABLESPOONS CILANTRO LEAVES (OPTIONAL)

3 CUPS SHREDDED, COOKED CHICKEN BREAST

**1.** In a medium bowl, whisk together the peanut butter, chicken broth, soy sauce, ginger juice, garlic, and red pepper flakes until smooth. Set aside.

**2.** Bring a large pot of lightly salted water to a boil over high heat. Add the linguine and cook until barely tender, about 9 minutes. Drain and rinse under cold running water until cool. Transfer to a large bowl. Add the peanut sauce and mix well. Add the scallions and optional cilantro and toss. Serve the pasta in individual pasta bowls, topped with the chicken.

**Poached Chicken Breasts:** This method gives moist, juicy chicken breasts. It may seem like 20 minutes isn't long enough to cook the breasts, but they will cook through as they stand in the hot cooking liquid.

Place two 8-ounce chicken breasts and ¼ teaspoon whole black peppercorns in a medium saucepan, and add enough lightly salted cold water to cover by 1 inch. Bring to a boil over medium heat. Reduce the heat to medium-low and simmer, uncovered, for 20 minutes. Remove from the heat and cover tightly. Let stand for 40 minutes. To use the chicken breasts for Cold Noodles with Chicken and Spicy Peanut Sauce, discard the skin and bones, and cut or pull the chicken breasts with the grain in thin shreds.

# Sicilian Spaghetti with Eggplant and Tuna

MAKES 4 TO 6 SERVINGS

When you dig into this gutsy-flavored pasta, words like *"Mama mia!"* will probably spring to your lips.
Pull out a bottle of hearty red wine, tuck a napkin under your chin, and go for it!

4 TABLESPOONS OLIVE OIL

1 SMALL EGGPLANT, CUT INTO ¾-INCH DICE (1 POUND)

1 MEDIUM ONION, CHOPPED

1 SMALL CARROT, CUT INTO ¼-INCH DICE

1 SMALL CELERY RIB, CUT INTO ¼-INCH DICE

2 GARLIC CLOVES, CHOPPED

ONE 28-OUNCE CAN TOMATOES IN JUICE, DRAINED,
   JUICES RESERVED, AND CHOPPED

2 TABLESPOONS TOMATO PASTE

1 TEASPOON DRIED BASIL

1 TEASPOON DRIED OREGANO

¼ TEASPOON CRUSHED HOT RED PEPPER FLAKES

TWO 6½-OUNCE CANS TUNA, PREFERABLY PACKED
   IN OLIVE OIL, DRAINED

½ CUP PITTED, CHOPPED BLACK MEDITERRANEAN OLIVES

3 TABLESPOONS BOTTLED CAPERS, RINSED, CHOPPED
   IF LARGE

1 POUND DRIED SPAGHETTI

**1.** In a large (12-inch) nonstick skillet, heat 3 tablespoons of the oil over medium-high heat until very hot, but not smoking. Add the eggplant and cook, turning occasionally, until browned on all sides, about 6 minutes. (The eggplant will absorb the oil, but resist the temptation to add more oil—the nonstick surface will keep the eggplant from scorching.) Transfer the eggplant to a plate and set aside.

**2.** Add the remaining 1 tablespoon oil to the skillet and reduce the heat to medium. Add the onion, carrot, celery, and garlic. Cook, stirring occasionally, until the vegetables soften, about 5 minutes. Stir in the tomatoes

with their juice, tomato paste, basil, oregano, and red pepper flakes. Bring to a simmer. Reduce the heat to medium-low and partially cover. Simmer until slightly thickened, about 25 minutes. Stir in the tuna, olives, and capers and cook just until heated through, about 5 minutes.

**3.** Meanwhile, bring a large pot of lightly salted water to a boil over high heat. Add the spaghetti and cook until barely tender, about 9 minutes. Drain well. Return the pasta to the cooking pot off heat, add the sauce, and toss well. Serve immediately.

# side dishes

THERE ARE MOVIES THAT ARE STAR TURNS, WHERE EVERYTHING DEPENDS ON HOW THE leading lady (or man) is featured. They're okay, but movies with an ensemble of performers, where every role is played with conviction, are a lot more interesting. I think of this phenomenon when I cook supper. Main courses are the stars, but without a good supporting cast, they're just another pretty face.

These vegetables and starchy side dishes will partner a wide variety of main courses. Everyone needs a good mashed potato recipe, and mine uses a spoonful of sour cream to add character (and essential richness). Many Mediterranean and Mexican dishes are better served with a polenta, so I've devised a chunky garlic and corn version. Here are recipes for the most popular side-dish vegetables, like broccoli, carrots, zucchini, spinach, cauliflower, and tomatoes. You'll find vegetables sautéed, grilled, baked, and roasted. And since it is so easy to make, I also included a recipe for a wonderfully tender cornbread to serve right out of the oven. Pass the butter and honey, please.

Infused oils are a great tool, cranking up the flavor of foods. While you can buy infused oils at a specialty food shop, it's easy to make your own. However, most recipes for homemade infused oil make a large amount that must be refrigerated and doesn't keep very long. I recently saw a recipe in a magazine that made 3 cups of herb oil, but kept for only one week in the refrigerator. Hey, I like parsley oil, but not 3 cups in one week! I suggest simply making the amount needed for each recipe.

# Grilled Artichokes with Lemon-Rosemary Marinade

MAKES 6 SERVINGS

*Grilled* artichokes? Sure, and they're terrific—slightly crispy, golden brown, and tender. I have seen recipes where they grill the whole darned raw artichoke until blackened. The method here is much easier to eat. Trimming the artichokes down to the heart may take some practice, but once you get the hang of it, it goes pretty quickly.

2 TABLESPOONS RED WINE VINEGAR

4 LARGE ARTICHOKES

¼ CUP PLUS 2 TABLESPOONS FRESH LEMON JUICE

2 GARLIC CLOVES, CRUSHED UNDER A KNIFE

2 TABLESPOONS CHOPPED FRESH ROSEMARY, OR

1 TEASPOON DRIED

½ TEASPOON SALT

¼ TEASPOON FRESHLY GROUND BLACK PEPPER

¾ CUP EXTRA-VIRGIN OLIVE OIL

**1.** Stir the vinegar into a large bowl of cold water. With a sharp paring knife, pare away the dark green peel from the stem and base of one of the artichokes. Dip the artichoke in the water. Snap off the dark green outer leaves to reveal the light green center cone of inner leaves. Cut off the top 1 inch of the artichoke. Using the tip of a spoon, dig out the purple leaves and hairy choke from the center, and cut the heart in half lengthwise. Place in the vinegar-water. Repeat with the remaining artichokes.

**2.** In a medium bowl, whisk together the lemon juice, garlic, rosemary, salt, and pepper. Whisk in the oil. Drain the artichokes and add to the marinade. Cover and let stand, mixing occasionally, for at least 15 minutes and up to 2 hours.

**3.** Build a charcoal fire in an outdoor grill and let the coals burn until covered with white ash. Or preheat a gas grill on medium heat. Remove the artichokes from the marinade and grill, turning occasionally, until lightly brown and tender, 10 to 15 minutes. Serve hot or at room temperature.

# Grilled Asparagus with Orange-Garlic Oil

MAKES 4 TO 6 SERVINGS

Grilled asparagus takes on a smoky flavor. It can be brushed with plain olive oil, but the infused variety is a nice way to gild the lily.

¼ CUP EXTRA-VIRGIN OLIVE OIL

ZEST OF ½ MEDIUM ORANGE, REMOVED WITH A
    VEGETABLE PEELER

2 GARLIC CLOVES, CRUSHED UNDER A KNIFE

¼ TEASPOON WHOLE BLACK PEPPERCORNS

1½ POUNDS ASPARAGUS, WOODY STEMS REMOVED

SALT

**1.** In a small saucepan, warm the oil, orange zest, garlic, and pepper over very low heat until fragrant and the garlic is surrounded by tiny bubbles, about 5 minutes. Do not cook the garlic until golden brown. Remove the saucepan from the heat and let stand and cool while preparing the grill.

**2.** Build a charcoal fire in an outdoor grill and let burn until hot. To use a gas grill, preheat on high. Lightly oil the grill grate.

**3.** Strain the oil into a small bowl. In a shallow dish, toss the asparagus with 2 tablespoons of the infused oil. Place the asparagus on the grill, with the spears running perpendicular to the grate (or use a perforated vegetable grill rack). Grill, turning halfway through, until lightly browned and tender, about 6 minutes. Serve with the remaining oil drizzled over the asparagus, if desired.

# Maple-Walnut Carrots

These are best made with pure maple syrup, not pancake syrup, which is no more than artificially flavored corn syrup.

6 MEDIUM CARROTS, CUT INTO ¼-INCH-THICK ROUNDS

¾ CUP BEEF BROTH, PREFERABLY HOMEMADE, OR USE LOW-SODIUM CANNED BROTH

3 TABLESPOONS PURE MAPLE SYRUP

1 TABLESPOON UNSALTED BUTTER

⅛ TEASPOON SALT

⅛ TEASPOON FRESHLY GROUND BLACK PEPPER

**1.** Place the carrots, broth, maple syrup, and butter in a medium nonstick skillet and bring to a boil over high heat. Partially cover and reduce the heat to medium. Simmer for 10 minutes.

**2.** Uncover the skillet and increase the heat to high. Boil, stirring occasionally, until the liquid evaporates and the carrots are glazed, about 7 minutes more. Season with the salt and pepper. Serve hot.

# Rosemary Roasted Cauliflower

Is there anyone out there who really *likes* soggy, bland, plain steamed cauliflower? Roasting gives this ugly duckling of the cruciferous set a deep flavor, especially when anointed with rosemary-scented oil.

3 TABLESPOONS EXTRA-VIRGIN OLIVE OIL

1 TABLESPOON CHOPPED FRESH ROSEMARY

2 GARLIC CLOVES, CRUSHED UNDER A KNIFE

1 MEDIUM CAULIFLOWER (1¾ POUNDS), TRIMMED AND
   CUT INTO 1-INCH FLORETS

¼ TEASPOON SALT

¼ TEASPOON FRESHLY GROUND BLACK PEPPER

**1.** In a small saucepan, warm the oil, rosemary, and garlic over low heat until fragrant and the garlic is surrounded by tiny bubbles, about 5 minutes. Do not cook the garlic until golden brown. Remove the saucepan from the heat and let stand and cool while preheating the oven.

**2.** Position a rack in the top third of the oven and preheat to 450°F. Lightly oil a 15 × 10 × 1-inch jelly roll pan.

**3.** Strain the oil into a small bowl. Place the cauliflower on the baking sheet and toss with the oil, seasoning with salt and pepper. Roast, stirring occasionally, until the cauliflower is tender and golden brown, about 40 minutes. Serve hot.

# Parmesan Polenta

Nothing is ever going to replace mashed potatoes, but with Mediterranean and Tex-Mex flavors, this polenta is a better-fitting side dish. Italian cooks tend to make their polenta on the plain side, but why not gussy it up?

1 TABLESPOON UNSALTED BUTTER

1 MEDIUM ONION, CHOPPED

2 GARLIC CLOVES, MINCED

2 CUPS WATER

1 TEASPOON SALT

1 CUP YELLOW STONE-GROUND CORNMEAL

1 CUP MILK

1 CUP FRESH OR THAWED FROZEN CORN KERNELS

½ CUP FRESHLY GRATED PARMESAN OR ROMANO CHEESE

**1.** In a medium, heavy-bottomed saucepan, heat the butter over medium heat. Add the onion and garlic and cook, stirring occasionally, until golden, about 5 minutes. Add the water and salt and bring to a boil over high heat.

**2.** In a small bowl, whisk the cornmeal with the milk until smooth. Whisk into the boiling liquid. Reduce the heat to low. Cook, whisking often, until the polenta is thick and begins to pull away from the sides of the saucepan, about 15 minutes. During the last 2 minutes, stir in the corn. Remove from the heat and stir in the cheese. Serve hot.

# Grilled New Potatoes in Garlicky Mustard Crust

### MAKES 6 TO 8 SERVINGS

Originally, I devised these spuds to go on Grilled Salmon Salad Niçoise (page 48), but I can guarantee you'll like them so much, you'll serve them with just about anything. The trick is to cut the parcooked potatoes into big chunks that won't fall through the grill grate.

2 POUNDS SMALL NEW POTATOES, SCRUBBED

½ CUP DIJON MUSTARD

¼ CUP OLIVE OIL

1 TABLESPOON FRESH ROSEMARY, OR 1 TEASPOON DRIED

1 TEASPOON YELLOW MUSTARD SEEDS

4 GARLIC CLOVES, CRUSHED THROUGH A PRESS

½ TEASPOON SALT

¼ TEASPOON FRESHLY GROUND BLACK PEPPER

**1.** In a large pot of salted water, cook the potatoes over high heat until just tender, about 20 minutes. Drain and rinse under cold water until cool enough to handle. Cut each potato in half.

**2.** In a large bowl, whisk together the mustard, oil, rosemary, mustard seeds, garlic, and salt. Add the potatoes and toss well to coat. Cover and let stand at room temperature for at least 15 minutes and up to 2 hours.

**3.** Build a hot fire in an outdoor grill and let the coals burn until covered with white ash. Let the coals burn until you can hold your hand over the coals for 2 to 3 seconds. Oil the grill grate well to keep the potatoes from sticking. Cook, turning occasionally, until tender and crusty on all sides, 8 to 10 minutes. Use a large spatula to transfer to a bowl.

To serve the potatoes with the Grilled Salmon Salad Niçoise, let the salmon cook for 5 minutes, then place the potatoes around the salmon so they will be finished at the same time.

# Southwestern Potato Pancakes

These are potato pancakes with attitude. Squeezing the liquid from the grated potatoes may sound fussy, but it makes the best pancakes, and when you do it, you'll see how simple it really is. Serve them as a side dish, or as a vegetarian main course with sour cream.

2 LARGE BAKING POTATOES, PEELED AND SHREDDED
(1¼ POUNDS TOTAL)

1 LARGE EGG, BEATEN

2 SCALLIONS, WHITE AND GREEN PARTS, MINCED

1 JALAPEÑO PEPPER, SEEDED AND MINCED

1 GARLIC CLOVE, CRUSHED THROUGH A PRESS

1 TEASPOON SALT

⅛ TEASPOON FRESHLY GROUND BLACK PEPPER

3 TABLESPOONS OLIVE OIL, PLUS MORE AS NEEDED

**1.** Preheat the oven to 200°F. A handful at a time, squeeze the potatoes over a large glass measuring cup or bowl to extract as much liquid as possible without trying to win any body-building awards. Place the squeezed potatoes in a medium bowl. Carefully pour off the cloudy liquid in the measuring cup, leaving the potato starch in the bottom of the cup. Scrape the starch into the potatoes. Add the egg, scallions, jalapeño, garlic, salt, and pepper and mix well.

**2.** In a large nonstick skillet, heat the oil over medium-high heat. Use ⅓ cup of the potato mixture for each pancake and cook, turning once, until golden brown on both sides, about 6 minutes. Transfer to a paper towel–lined baking sheet and keep warm in the oven. To make the remaining pancakes, drain off the accumulated liquid in the potato mixture, and add more oil to skillet as needed. Serve warm.

# Smashed Potatoes with Sour Cream and Scallions

MAKES 4 TO 6 SERVINGS

The skins on red or white are tender enough to eat, packed with fiber and vitamins, and tasty, too. Restaurants around the country have figured this out, where they call peel-on potatoes "smashed," not "mashed" potatoes. Can I have these every night for dinner, please?

3 POUNDS MEDIUM RED- OR WHITE-SKINNED POTATOES, SCRUBBED, UNPEELED

3 TABLESPOONS UNSALTED BUTTER

3 SCALLIONS, WHITE AND GREEN PARTS, CHOPPED

½ CUP SOUR CREAM, AT ROOM TEMPERATURE

½ CUP MILK, AT ROOM TEMPERATURE, AS NEEDED

½ TEASPOON SALT

¼ TEASPOON FRESHLY GROUND WHITE PEPPER

**1.** Cut the potatoes into 2-inch chunks and place in a large pot. Add enough lightly salted cold water to cover by 2 inches. Bring to a boil over high heat. Reduce the heat to medium-low and cook until the potatoes are tender when pierced with the tip of a knife, about 25 minutes.

**2.** Meanwhile, heat the butter in a medium skillet over medium heat. Add the scallions and cook, stirring occasionally, until lightly browned, about 3 minutes. Set aside.

**3.** Drain the potatoes well. Return to the still-warm cooking pot. Using a hand-held electric mixer on low speed (or a potato masher), mash the potatoes with the scallions and their butter and the sour cream, gradually adding milk as needed to get the desired consistency. Season with the salt and pepper. Serve immediately.

# Ginger-Sesame Spinach

When you want a simple, fresh-tasting green vegetable, turn to this recipe. I serve it often as a base for Park's Salmon Teriyaki on page 47. It's best with delicate, light flat spinach leaves, not the curly, dark variety.

2 POUNDS FRESH SPINACH, TOUGH STEMS REMOVED

2 TEASPOONS SESAME SEEDS

1 TABLESPOON VEGETABLE OIL

2 TEASPOONS GRATED FRESH GINGER (USE THE LARGE HOLES ON A BOX GRATER)

1 GARLIC CLOVE, CRUSHED THROUGH A PRESS

**1.** Fill a sink or large bowl with lukewarm water. Submerge the spinach and agitate it well to remove all grit. Taste a piece to be sure it's clean, and repeat the procedure if necessary. Lift the spinach out of the water and transfer to a large colander, leaving the grit in the bottom of the sink. Do not dry the spinach.

**2.** Heat a large, dry skillet over medium heat. Add the sesame seeds and cook, stirring often, until toasted, about 1 minute. Transfer to a bowl and set aside.

**3.** Add the oil to the skillet and heat. Add the ginger and garlic and stir until fragrant, about 30 seconds. In batches, add the spinach, stirring until the first batch is wilted before adding the next. Cook until the spinach is tender through, about 5 minutes.

**4.** Transfer to a colander and press gently to remove excess moisture. Serve, sprinkled with the sesame seeds.

Be sure to rinse fresh spinach well—if it's sandy, you'll regret it. For that reason, I have been specific about how best to wash the leaves. Lukewarm water will loosen grit better than cold. And don't spin-dry spinach if it is going to be served hot, as the water clinging to the leaves will create steam for cooking.

# Two-Squash Sauté with Oregano and Lemon

**MAKES 4 TO 6 SERVINGS**

Yellow summer squash and green zucchini look great together. Even with such a simple dish as this, there is an essential cooking secret. Don't salt the squash until after it is cooked, otherwise it will give off liquid and not brown properly. For a richer variation, delete the lemon zest and top the sautéed squash with 1/3 cup crumbled feta cheese.

2 TABLESPOONS OLIVE OIL

1 LARGE ZUCCHINI, SCRUBBED, CUT INTO 1/2-INCH DICE

1 LARGE YELLOW SQUASH, SCRUBBED, CUT INTO
   1/2-INCH DICE

1 GARLIC CLOVE, MINCED

1/2 TEASPOON DRIED OREGANO

1/4 TEASPOON CRUSHED HOT RED PEPPER FLAKES

GRATED ZEST OF 1 LEMON

1/4 TEASPOON SALT

**1.** In a large (12-inch) nonstick skillet, heat the oil over medium-high heat. Add the zucchini and yellow squash and cook, stirring occasionally, until tender and lightly browned, about 8 minutes. During the last 2 minutes, stir in the garlic, oregano, and red pepper flakes.

**2.** Remove from the heat and stir in the lemon zest and salt. Serve hot.

When cooking zucchini or summer squash, bring out the vegetable brush and give it a good scrubbing first before cutting up. It's another one of those vegetables that seems pristine at first glance, but often has a fine gritty coating that needs to be removed.

# Grilled Beefsteak Tomatoes with Basil Oil

MAKES 4 SERVINGS

Drizzled with a freshly prepared basil oil, this is a sexy way to dress up plain grilled tomatoes. It's no secret that tomatoes are at their best in the height of summer, but the imported Israeli or Holland tomatoes are a fine substitute. Just stay away from the anemic pink ones.

¼ CUP PACKED BASIL LEAVES

¼ CUP PLUS 1 TABLESPOON EXTRA-VIRGIN OLIVE OIL

2 LARGE BEEFSTEAK TOMATOES, HALVED HORIZONTALLY

¼ TEASPOON SALT

⅛ TEASPOON FRESHLY GROUND BLACK PEPPER

**1.** Bring a medium saucepan of water to a boil over high heat. Add the basil leaves and cook for 15 seconds. Drain in a wire sieve, rinse under cold water, and press gently to remove excess water.

**2.** In a blender, puree the basil with ¼ cup of the oil. Set aside.

**3.** Build a charcoal fire in an outdoor grill and let the coals burn until covered with white ash and medium-hot. Or preheat a gas grill on high and adjust to medium. Lightly oil the grill.

**4.** Brush the cut sides of the tomatoes with the remaining 1 tablespoon oil and season with the salt and pepper. Grill, cut sides down, until lightly browned, about 2 minutes. Turn and grill until the tomatoes are just heated through, 2 to 3 minutes. Serve the tomatoes drizzled with the basil oil. Serve hot or at room temperature.

# Spinach-Stuffed Tomatoes

MAKES 6 SERVINGS

I love creamed spinach. I love baked tomatoes. I love spinach-stuffed baked tomatoes. To save time, use frozen spinach—it's a perfectly fine convenience food.

1 TABLESPOON UNSALTED BUTTER

2 TABLESPOONS MINCED SHALLOTS

1 GARLIC CLOVE, MINCED

TWO 9-OUNCE BOXES THAWED FROZEN CHOPPED
    SPINACH, SQUEEZED TO REMOVE EXCESS MOISTURE

1 CUP HEAVY CREAM

A FEW GRATINGS OF FRESH NUTMEG

¼ TEASPOON SALT

¼ TEASPOON FRESHLY GROUND BLACK PEPPER

6 MEDIUM TOMATOES, CUT IN HALF HORIZONTALLY,
    INSIDES SCOOPED OUT TO MAKE TOMATO SHELLS

3 TABLESPOONS DRY BREAD CRUMBS

1 TABLESPOON OLIVE OIL

**1.** Position a rack in the top part of the oven and pre-heat to 400°F. Lightly oil a 13 × 9-inch baking dish.

**2.** In a medium nonstick skillet, melt the butter over medium heat. Add the shallots and garlic and cook, stirring often, until softened, about 2 minutes. Add the spinach and cook until heated through, about 2 minutes. Stir in the cream and bring to a boil. Cook until the cream is almost evaporated, about 5 minutes. Season with the nutmeg, salt, and pepper.

**3.** Fill the tomato shells with the spinach mixture. Sprinkle the tops with the bread crumbs and drizzle with the oil. Bake until the tops are browned, about 30 minutes. Serve hot.

To quickly thaw frozen spinach, use your microwave oven. Or place the spinach in a wire sieve and rinse under hot water until thawed.

# Oven-Roasted, Chile-Kissed Yams

MAKES 4 TO 6 SERVINGS

These are a perfect side dish for grilled pork chops or baked ham. (Keep them in mind when you need an unusual sweet potato side dish for the holiday turkey.) If you have any leftovers, blend them into a soup with a little chicken broth and milk, and heat for a quick lunch.

4 LARGE ORANGE-FLESHED SWEET POTATOES (YAMS),
    PEELED AND CUT INTO 1-INCH CUBES (2 POUNDS TOTAL)
2 TABLESPOONS UNSALTED BUTTER
2 TABLESPOONS OLIVE OIL

3 GARLIC CLOVES, CRUSHED UNDER A KNIFE
½ TEASPOON SALT
1 TABLESPOON GROUND MILD CHILE PEPPER, SUCH AS
    CHIMAYO, OR CHILI POWDER

**1.** Position a rack in the top third of the oven and preheat to 400°F. Lightly oil a 15 × 10-inch baking dish.

**2.** Bring a large pot of lightly salted water to a boil over high heat. Add the sweet potatoes and parboil for 5 minutes. Drain and rinse under cold running water. Place the sweet potatoes in the prepared baking dish.

**3.** Meanwhile, in a small saucepan, heat the butter, oil, and garlic until the garlic is bubbling around the edges but not browned. Strain over the sweet potatoes, season with the salt, and toss.

**4.** Bake, turning the sweet potatoes occasionally with a metal spatula, until tender and browned, about 1 hour. During the last 5 minutes, sprinkle with the ground chile. Serve hot.

Depending on where you live, orange-fleshed sweet potatoes can be called yams. Jewel yams are an especially good variety with a firm texture and not-too-sweet flavor. True yams, popular with Caribbean cooks, have a scaled, brown peel, and are tubers similar to yucca or cassava. True sweet potatoes, available at Hispanic markets, have a creamy yellow flesh and are also called *batatas*. Although *batatas* are not as sweet, they can be used in any orange-fleshed sweet potato recipe.

*continued*

Many supermarkets are now selling ground chile peppers without any additional seasonings. (Traditional chili powder will usually include ground cumin and sometimes oregano and garlic powder, because it is assumed it will be used to season a pot of Texas-style meat chili.) If at all possible, use ground Chimayo or Hatch chile powder, from the region in New Mexico that produces a particularly sweet and mild chile pepper.

# Chunky Corn and Chile Cornbread

Sometimes, nothing rounds out a meal like a wedge of piping-hot cornbread. This is an especially melt-in-your-mouth recipe, thanks to the tenderizing effect of yogurt in baked goods.

1 CUP ALL-PURPOSE FLOUR

1 CUP YELLOW CORNMEAL, PREFERABLY STONE-GROUND

2 TABLESPOONS SUGAR

¾ TEASPOON BAKING SODA

¾ TEASPOON SALT

1 CUP PLAIN LOW-FAT YOGURT

½ CUP MILK

2 LARGE EGGS, BEATEN

¼ CUP (½ STICK) UNSALTED BUTTER, MELTED

1 CUP FRESH OR THAWED FROZEN CORN KERNELS

1 JALAPEÑO PEPPER, SEEDED AND MINCED

**1.** Position a rack in the center of the oven and pre-heat to 375°F. Lightly butter a 9-inch square baking pan.

**2.** In a large bowl, whisk the flour, cornmeal, sugar, baking soda, and salt to combine. Make a well in the center. In a small bowl, whisk the yogurt, milk, and eggs to combine. Pour into the well, add the butter, and stir with a wooden spoon just until moistened and combined. Gently fold in the corn and jalapeño. Do not overmix. Scrape into the prepared pan and smooth the top.

**3.** Bake until a toothpick inserted in the center comes out clean, about 30 minutes. Serve hot, warm, or at room temperature.

# desserts

Okay, I'll admit it. I am not much of a dessert maker. I love to eat desserts, but a good baker needs a certain amount of patience. I have many good qualities, but patience is not one of them.

So I have acquainted myself with easy dessert recipes that even I like to make. Instead of *not* baking a cake because I want to avoid cleaning up a sinkful of bowls, I'll whip up a one-bowl batter. No one will feel cheated by my Peach Preserves Cake with Bourbon Soak. Likewise, most cookies frustrate me because it takes too long to portion out the dough. No problem—I can make a pan of bar cookies in half the time and trouble. If I don't feel like taking out my ice cream machine, I can still make Strawberry-Lemonade Granita in the freezer.

Many of these desserts are so easy to make that you can have them for a weeknight supper. And most make more than just a few servings, so you'll have extra for afternoon pick-me-ups, midnight snacks, and lunch boxes. If you have a lot of extras, just bring them into the office and share with your fellow workers. Don't be surprised if you're elected Employee of the Month.

# Zucchini and Orange Pound Cake

One of the easiest cakes around, and one of the best. Most American's wouldn't think of using olive oil for making a cake, but it is a natural for this zucchini loaf, spiked with citrus flavor. Use regular (previously known as "pure") olive oil, as the extra-virgin is too heavy. Low in fat it isn't, but it will please any poor souls in your group that are concerned about cholesterol. The cake is wonderful on its own, but even better when served with a spoonful of fresh berries.

1½ CUPS ALL-PURPOSE FLOUR

½ TEASPOON SALT

½ TEASPOON BAKING SODA

¼ TEASPOON BAKING POWDER

¼ TEASPOON GROUND NUTMEG

1 LARGE EGG, PLUS 1 LARGE EGG WHITE, AT ROOM
    TEMPERATURE

1 CUP GRANULATED SUGAR

¾ CUP REGULAR (PURE, NOT EXTRA-VIRGIN) OLIVE OIL

1⅓ CUPS GRATED ZUCCHINI (ABOUT 1 LARGE ZUCCHINI)

GRATED ZEST OF 1 ORANGE

3 TABLESPOONS CONFECTIONERS' SUGAR, SIFTED

3 TABLESPOONS FRESH ORANGE JUICE

**1.** Preheat the oven to 350°F. With a paper towel, lightly oil a 8 × 4-inch loaf pan. Dust the inside of the pan with flour and tap out the excess.

**2.** Sift the flour, salt, baking soda, baking powder, and nutmeg into a small bowl and set aside.

**3.** In a medium bowl, using an electric mixer on high speed, beat the egg and egg white until thickened and light in color, about 1 minute. In 3 additions, beat in the sugar. In 3 additions, beat in the oil. Beat in the zucchini and orange zest. On low speed, beat in the flour mixture, just until blended. Pour into the pan and smooth the top.

**4.** Bake until the cracks in the top of the cake look dry and a toothpick inserted in the center comes out clean, 50 minutes to 1 hour. Cool on a wire cake rack for 5 minutes. Unmold onto the cake rack.

**5.** In a small bowl, stir the confectioners' sugar with the orange juice to make a thin glaze. Brush the glaze over the top and sides of the cake. Cool the cake completely.

# Peach Preserves Cake
# with Bourbon Soak

### MAKES 12 SERVINGS

Peach preserves may seem like an unlikely ingredient for a cake, but they pack fruity flavor into every slice—you'll see chunks of fruit suspended in the cake. Just be sure to use preserves, not jam (which is made from pureed fruit) or jelly (which is thickened juice without fruit chunks). This makes a big ol' cake, so unless you have an enormous family or appetite, expect to have a goodly amount of leftovers. No bourbon? Use dark rum, brandy, or Cognac. Kids around? Skip the glaze. It's still delicious.

3 CUPS ALL-PURPOSE FLOUR

1 TEASPOON BAKING SODA

1 TEASPOON GROUND CINNAMON

½ TEASPOON SALT

¾ CUP PLAIN LOWFAT YOGURT

¼ CUP MILK

½ TEASPOON VANILLA EXTRACT

¾ CUP (1½ STICKS) UNSALTED BUTTER, AT ROOM
   TEMPERATURE

1½ CUPS GRANULATED SUGAR

4 LARGE EGGS, AT ROOM TEMPERATURE

2 CUPS PEACH PRESERVES

1½ CUPS (6 OUNCES) COARSELY CHOPPED PECANS

⅓ CUP CONFECTIONERS' SUGAR

⅓ CUP BOURBON

**1.** Preheat the oven to 350°F. Butter and flour a 10-cup fluted tube pan and tap out the excess flour.

**2.** Sift the flour, baking soda, cinnamon, and salt through a wire strainer onto a piece of waxed paper, and set aside. In a measuring cup, mix the yogurt, milk, and vanilla, and set aside.

**3.** In a large bowl, using a handheld electric mixer set at high speed, beat the butter and sugar until light in color and texture, about 2 minutes. One at a time, beat

in the eggs. Reduce the mixer to low. One-third at a time, alternately add the flour mixture and yogurt mixture, beating after each addition and scraping down the sides of the bowl. The batter will be thick. Beat in the peach preserves, and then the pecans. Transfer the batter to the prepared pan, smoothing the top.

**4.** Bake until a toothpick inserted in the center of the cake comes out clean, about 1¼ hours. Let stand in the pan for 10 minutes. Invert onto a wire cake rack and unmold.

**5.** In a small bowl, dissolve the confectioners' sugar in the bourbon. Brush the syrup all over the warm cake. Cool completely.

**Variation:**

Try other preserves, such as apricot, blackberry, and raspberry, or combine leftover preserves to make your own unique version.

# Secret Ingredient
# Chocolate Layer Cake

A layer cake may not sound like an easy dessert, but wait until you try this tall, chocolately miracle. The secret ingredient is mayonnaise—which doesn't sound as strange as it might when you consider that it is mostly eggs and oil, two common ingredients in cake batter. The frosting is simple too, and makes a really thick layer of icing, for all of you icing lovers out there.

**FOR THE CAKE**

2 CUPS ALL-PURPOSE FLOUR

1 CUP GRANULATED SUGAR

⅓ CUP PLUS 1 TABLESPOON REGULAR (NOT DUTCH-
   PROCESS) COCOA POWDER, SUCH AS HERSHEY'S

2 TEASPOONS BAKING SODA

¼ TEASPOON SALT

1 CUP MAYONNAISE (NOT REDUCED FAT)

1 CUP COLD STRONG BREWED COFFEE

1 TEASPOON VANILLA EXTRACT

**FOR THE FROSTING**

2 CUPS CONFECTIONERS' SUGAR

½ CUP REGULAR COCOA POWDER, SUCH AS HERSHEY'S

⅓ CUP UNSALTED BUTTER, AT ROOM TEMPERATURE

⅔ CUP HEAVY CREAM, APPROXIMATELY

1 TEASPOON VANILLA EXTRACT

**1.** To make the cake, position a rack in the center of the oven and preheat to 350°F. Lightly butter two 8-inch round cake pans. Dust the insides of the pans with flour, shaking out the excess. Line the bottoms with waxed paper. Sift the flour, sugar, cocoa, baking soda, and salt onto a piece of waxed paper and set aside.

**2.** In a large bowl, whisk the mayonnaise, coffee, and vanilla until combined. Add the dry ingredients and whisk until smooth. Transfer to the prepared pans and smooth the tops.

**3.** Bake until a toothpick inserted into the centers comes out clean, 20 to 25 minutes. Cool on wire cake racks for 10 minutes. Invert the cakes to unmold, remove the waxed paper, then cool completely, right sides up.

**4.** To make the frosting, sift the confectioners' sugar and cocoa into a medium bowl. In a large bowl, using a handheld electric mixer set at medium speed, beat the butter until creamy. Gradually beat in the cocoa mixture, alternating with enough of the cream to make a smooth, spreadable frosting. Beat in the vanilla.

**5.** Dab a tablespoon of frosting on a serving plate, and place one cake layer, upside down, on the frosting. (This "glues" the cake onto the plate.) Spread about ³/₄ cup of frosting on the cake layer, then top with the second layer, right side up. Frost the top, then the sides, of the cake. Serve at room temperature.

# Chocolate Banana Loaf

I just can't resist dunking a thick slab of this cake into a glass of cold milk. It's a versatile cake that's delicious any time of day—for breakfast with coffee, at lunchtime (it's the perfect texture for packing in a lunch box), for an afternoon snack, or for a supper dessert with ice cream and hot chocolate sauce.

1 OUNCE UNSWEETENED CHOCOLATE, FINELY CHOPPED

½ CUP MILK

1 TEASPOON CIDER VINEGAR

2 CUPS ALL-PURPOSE FLOUR

2 TABLESPOONS DUTCH-PROCESS COCOA POWDER,
    SUCH AS DRÖSTE (SEE OPPOSITE PAGE)

¾ TEASPOON BAKING SODA

½ TEASPOON BAKING POWDER

¼ TEASPOON SALT

½ CUP (1 STICK) UNSALTED BUTTER, AT ROOM TEMPERATURE

1½ CUPS SUGAR

2 LARGE EGGS, AT ROOM TEMPERATURE

1 TEASPOON VANILLA EXTRACT

1 CUP (ABOUT 2 MEDIUM) MASHED, RIPE BANANAS (SEE NOTE)

1 CUP (4 OUNCES) COARSELY CHOPPED WALNUTS

**1.** Position a rack in the center of the oven and preheat to 350°F. Lightly butter the inside of a 9 × 5-inch loaf pan. Dust with flour, tapping out excess flour. Line the bottom of the pan with waxed paper.

**2.** In the top part of a double boiler over hot, not simmering, water, melt the chocolate. Or melt the chocolate in a small bowl in a microwave oven at medium (50 percent) power until it looks shiny, about 1 minute, then stir until melted. Let the chocolate cool until tepid.

**3.** In a glass measuring cup, combine the milk and vinegar. Sift the flour, cocoa, baking soda, baking powder, and salt onto a piece of waxed paper.

**4.** In a large bowl, using a handheld electric mixer at high speed, cream the butter and sugar until light in consistency and color, about 2 minutes. One at a time, beat in the eggs, then the vanilla. Add the cooled chocolate and bananas and beat until smooth. Alternating in thirds, add the flour mixture and milk, beating well after each addition and scraping down the sides of the bowl as needed. Stir in the walnuts. Transfer to the prepared pan and smooth the top.

**5.** Bake until a toothpick inserted in the center comes out clean, 1¼ to 1½ hours. Cool the cake on a wire cake pan for 15 minutes. Invert the cake to unmold, remove the waxed paper, and cool completely, right side up.

**Note:** The bananas should be ripe and well-freckled, but not so ripe that they smell alcoholic.

Dutch-process cocoa is a special process that originated in the Netherlands. "Dutching" alkalizes the cocoa to reduce its acidity (cocoa's high acidity can wreak havoc with a recipe's leavening), and gives the finished product a deeper brown color. If the box isn't clearly marked on the front, check on the side panel to see if it says "Dutch-process" or "alkalized." Hershey's brown box cocoa is nonalkalized, but they have a "European-style" in a silver box that is. Dutch-process cocoa can be found in specialty food shops and many supermarkets (look in the imported foods section if it isn't with the baking chocolate or regular cocoa powder). Dutch-process isn't especially better than regular cocoa powder, only different. It isn't always interchangeable with nonalkalized cocoa, so if a recipe specifies "Dutch-process," use it.

# Blueberry Scone-Cake with Strawberries

Scones are kissing cousins to biscuits, which are related to shortcakes, so it didn't take long to figure out that scones would make pretty good strawberry shortcakes, too. These have lots of butter for flakiness, buttermilk for tenderness, and blueberries for the heck of it.

**FOR THE STRAWBERRIES**

2 PINTS FRESH STRAWBERRIES, HULLED AND SLICED

2 TABLESPOONS SUGAR

**FOR THE SCONE-CAKE**

2 CUPS ALL-PURPOSE FLOUR

2 TABLESPOONS SUGAR

2 TEASPOONS BAKING POWDER

GRATED ZEST OF 1 LEMON

½ TEASPOON SALT

¼ TEASPOON BAKING SODA

½ CUP (1 STICK) UNSALTED BUTTER, CHILLED,
    CUT INTO ½-INCH CUBES

¾ CUP BUTTERMILK, PLUS EXTRA FOR BRUSHING

1 CUP FRESH OR FROZEN BLUEBERRIES

**FOR THE CREAM**

1 CUP HEAVY CREAM

2 TABLESPOONS SUGAR

1 TEASPOON VANILLA EXTRACT

**1.** To prepare the strawberries, mix the berries and sugar well in a medium bowl until the berries begin to give off some juices. Cover and refrigerate until ready to serve.

**2.** To make the scone-cake, preheat the oven to 400°F. Sift 1³/₄ cups flour, 1 tablespoon sugar, the baking powder, zest, salt, and baking soda into a medium bowl. Using a pastry blender or 2 forks, cut and press the butter into the flour mixture until most of the pieces are the size of small peas or smaller (but not the

"cornmeal" size that some recipes may indicate). Stir in the buttermilk to make a soft dough.

**3.** In a small bowl, toss the blueberries with the remaining ¹/₄ cup flour. Stir into the dough until combined. Gather up the dough and pat out into an 8-inch round on an ungreased baking sheet. Using a sharp knife, cut the round into 8 wedges, but do not separate them. Brush the top of the round with a little extra buttermilk, and sprinkle with the remaining 1 tablespoon sugar.

**4.** Bake until the top is golden brown and a toothpick inserted near the center comes out clean, 20 to 25 minutes. Cool on the baking sheet.

**5.** When ready to serve, beat the cream, sugar, and vanilla until stiff. Place a wedge of scone-cake on each dessert plate, and top with a spoonful of berries with their juices and a dollop of whipped cream.

# Free-Form Gingered Apple Galette

Good ol' American pies are great, but sometimes I like the free-form opportunities offered by the French *galette*—line a round of dough with slices of fruit, then fold the sides up and over to make a crust. If you use store-bought pie pastry, it is very quick to make, but if you have the time, use homemade crust.

ONE 7½-OUNCE ROUND REFRIGERATED PREPARED PIE
    CRUST, OR USE HOMEMADE *GALETTE* DOUGH
    (SEE BELOW)
2 LARGE GOLDEN DELICIOUS APPLES, PEELED,
    QUARTERED LENGTHWISE, CORED, AND CUT INTO
    LONG ½-INCH-THICK SLICES
2 TABLESPOONS FINELY CHOPPED CRYSTALLIZED GINGER

1 TABLESPOON FRESH LEMON JUICE
3 TABLESPOONS SUGAR
3 TABLESPOONS ALL-PURPOSE FLOUR
1 TABLESPOON HEAVY CREAM OR MILK
1 TABLESPOON CHILLED UNSALTED BUTTER,
    CUT INTO SMALL PIECES

**1.** Position a rack in the center of the oven and preheat to 400°F. On a lightly floured surface, roll out the dough (if necessary) into a 10-inch round. Transfer to an ungreased rimless baking sheet or a pizza pan.

**2.** In a medium bowl, toss the apples with the ginger, lemon juice, 2 tablespoons sugar, and 1 tablespoon flour. Leaving a 2-inch border, arrange the largest apple slices in a circle, overlapping them slightly, then fill the center with a mound of the smaller slices. Fold the crust over to partially cover the apples, gently pleating the crust as needed. Brush the crust lightly with the cream, then drizzle the remainder over the apples.

**3.** In a small bowl, mix the remaining 2 tablespoons flour and 1 tablespoon sugar with the butter. Rub the mixture between your fingers until well combined and crumbly. Crumble over the apples.

**4.** Bake until the crust is golden and the apple juices are bubbling, about 35 minutes. Cool on the pan. Serve warm or at room temperature.

**Homemade *Galette* Dough:** In a measuring cup, mix ¼ cup ice water with 1 large egg yolk. In a medium bowl, combine 1 cup all-purpose flour, 1½ tablespoons sugar, and ⅛ teaspoon salt. Add 6 tablespoons chilled unsalted butter, cut into ½-inch pieces. Using a pastry blender, cut the butter into the flour until it forms coarse crumbs. Tossing with a fork, gradually add enough of the egg mixture until moistened. Gather up dough and pinch to see if it holds together. You may need more or less of the liquid to get the right consistency. Gather up the dough into a thick disk. Wrap in waxed paper. Chill for at least 1 hour or up to 1 day. Let soften slightly at room temperature before rolling out.

Golden Delicious apples are great for pies and tarts— they are just tart enough and hold their shape when baked. Granny Smiths, although tarter and firmer, are another good choice, or mix them up. Stay away from McIntosh, which makes better applesauce than pie filling.

# Peanut Butter and Banana Pie

MAKES 6 TO 8 SERVINGS

Here's a hassle-free dessert that's perfect for summer picnics. It's so easy it seems like a sin. That is, until you taste it, then you'll *really* know what sin is.

**FOR THE CRUST**

1 CUP CHOCOLATE WAFER COOKIE CRUMBS
   (ABOUT 5 OUNCES)
¼ CUP GRANULATED SUGAR
¼ CUP (½ STICK) UNSALTED BUTTER, MELTED

**FOR THE FILLING**

11 OUNCES CREAM CHEESE, AT ROOM TEMPERATURE
¾ CUP CREAMY PEANUT BUTTER
1¼ CUPS PLUS 2 TABLESPOONS HEAVY CREAM
1 CUP CONFECTIONERS' SUGAR
2 RIPE BANANAS, THINLY SLICED
*GARNISH:* ¼ CUP CHOCOLATE-COVERED PEANUTS,
   COARSELY CHOPPED (OPTIONAL)

**1.** To make the crust, position a rack in the center of the oven and preheat to 350°F. In a medium bowl, mix the cookie crumbs, sugar, and butter until the crumbs are well moistened. Press evenly into the bottom and up the sides of an ungreased, 9-inch pie plate. Bake until the crust is set, 10 to 12 minutes. Cool completely on a wire cake rack.

**2.** To make the filling, in a large bowl, using a hand-held electric mixer at high speed, beat the cream cheese, peanut butter, and 2 tablespoons heavy cream until smooth and creamy. Gradually beat in the confectioners' sugar.

**3.** In a chilled, medium bowl, beat the remaining 1¼ cups heavy cream until soft peaks form. Fold into the cream cheese mixture until combined. Layer the banana slices into the prepared pie crust. Spread the filling over the bananas. Cover with plastic wrap and refrigerate until firm, at least 3 hours or overnight. Sprinkle with the chocolate-covered peanuts, if desired, and serve.

# Chocolate-Raspberry Brownies

MAKES 6 LARGE BROWNIES

Are these the best brownies in the world? This is one of life's big questions, up there with, Are the Cowboys a better team than the Oilers? Thick, chewy, fudgy, with gems of raspberries tucked into the batter, the lily gets gilded with a milk chocolate icing. My trick of lining the pan with foil allows you to lift out the brownie in one big piece—no more digging to get that first corner brownie out of the pan.

½ CUP (1 STICK) UNSALTED BUTTER, CUT INTO PIECES

3 OUNCES BITTERSWEET CHOCOLATE, FINELY CHOPPED

2 OUNCES UNSWEETENED CHOCOLATE, FINELY CHOPPED

1 CUP FIRMLY PACKED LIGHT BROWN SUGAR

2 LARGE EGGS, AT ROOM TEMPERATURE

2 TABLESPOONS LIGHT CORN SYRUP

1 TEASPOON VANILLA EXTRACT

1¼ CUPS ALL-PURPOSE FLOUR

¼ TEASPOON BAKING SODA

¼ TEASPOON SALT

6 OUNCES FRESH OR FROZEN RASPBERRIES

6 OUNCES MILK CHOCOLATE, FINELY CHOPPED

**1.** Position a rack in the center of the oven and preheat to 350°F. Fold a 16-inch-long piece of foil lengthwise to fit the bottom on an 8-inch square baking pan, letting the ends of the foil hang over the sides as handles. Lightly butter the foil and sides of the pan, dust with flour, and tap out the excess.

**2.** In a large saucepan, melt the butter over medium heat. Remove the pan from the heat and add the bittersweet and unsweetened chocolates. Let stand until the chocolates soften, about 3 minutes. Whisk until smooth. Whisk in the brown sugar. One at a time, whisk in the eggs, then the corn syrup and vanilla.

**3.** In a small bowl, combine the flour, baking soda, and salt, then sift the dry ingredients over the choco-

late mixture. Using a rubber spatula, fold together until combined. The batter will be thick. Fold in the raspberries, and although some of them will break, try to keep them as whole as possible.

**4.** Spread evenly into the prepared baking pan. Bake until a toothpick inserted in the center comes out with a moist crumb, about 30 minutes. Do not overbake. Place the pan on a wire cake rack. Sprinkle the milk chocolate on top of the warm brownie. Let stand until the chocolate softens, about 5 minutes. Using a cake spatula, thinly spread the milk chocolate over the brownies. Cool completely. Run a knife around the inside of the pan, then lift up on the foil handles to remove from the pan. Cut into 6 bars.

# S'Mores Bars

MAKES 8 BIG BARS

Want to see a dessert disappear? Make these chewy bars—they're perfect for snacks, lunch boxes, and any time you just want to feel good. The pleasures of S'mores being well known, it should take little encouragement to turn graham crackers, milk chocolate, and marshmallows into a brownielike cookie. They are really a snap to make, but you may want to have a kitchen timer handy as each layer gets baked for a few minutes before adding the next, and it's easy to lose track (especially when you have a three-year-old in the house, as I do).

2¼ CUPS GRAHAM CRACKER CRUMBS (8 OUNCES)

½ CUP (1 STICK) PLUS 3 TABLESPOONS UNSALTED
    BUTTER, MELTED

¼ CUP SUGAR

1 LARGE EGG WHITE, BEATEN UNTIL FOAMY

ONE 11½-OUNCE BAG MILK CHOCOLATE CHIPS (2 CUPS)

5 OUNCES MINI-MARSHMALLOWS (2½ CUPS)

**1.** Position a rack in the center of the oven and preheat to 350°F. Fold a 16-inch-long piece of foil lengthwise to fit the bottom on a 11 × 17-inch baking pan, letting the ends of the foil hang over the sides as handles. Lightly butter the foil and sides of the pan.

**2.** In a medium bowl, mix the graham cracker crumbs, melted butter, sugar, and egg white until well moistened. Set aside 1 cup of the crumbs. Press the remaining crumbs firmly and evenly into the prepared pan.

**3.** Bake until the crust looks dry and set, about 15 minutes. Remove from the oven and sprinkle with the chocolate chips. Bake until the chips look shiny and are beginning to soften, about 2 minutes. Remove from the oven and arrange the marshmallows evenly over the chips. Return to the oven and bake until the marshmallows puff slightly, about 5 minutes. Sprinkle with the reserved crumbs, pressing gently into the marshmallows to adhere. Bake until the marshmallows are golden brown, about 5 minutes. Cool completely on a wire cake rack. Run a knife around the inside of the pan, then lift up on the foil handles to remove from the pan. To serve, cut into 8 bars.

# Apricot and Almond Crumble Bars

Does anyone really own a functioning cookie jar anymore?
These sweet-tart, old-fashioned bars will put yours back into action.

⅔ CUP SLICED ALMONDS, NATURAL OR BLANCHED

½ CUP SUGAR

¾ CUP (1½ STICKS) UNSALTED BUTTER, SOFTENED

¼ TEASPOON ALMOND EXTRACT

1½ CUPS ALL-PURPOSE FLOUR

½ TEASPOON BAKING POWDER

1 CUP HIGH-QUALITY APRICOT PRESERVES

**1.** Position a rack in the center of the oven and preheat to 350°F. Fold a 16-inch-long piece of foil lengthwise to fit the bottom of an 11 × 7-inch baking pan, letting the ends of the foil hang over the sides as handles. Lightly butter the foil and sides of the pan.

**2.** In a food processor, pulse the almonds with 2 tablespoons sugar until processed almost into a powder. Set aside.

**3.** In a medium bowl, using a handheld electric mixer on high speed, beat the butter and remaining 6 tablespoons sugar until light in color, about 2 minutes. Beat in the almond extract. Using a wooden spoon, stir in the flour, ground almonds, and baking powder. Press half of the dough firmly and evenly into the prepared pan. Spread the preserves over the crust. Crumble the remaining dough as evenly as possible over the preserves.

**4.** Bake until the crumb topping is golden brown, about 25 minutes. Cool completely on a wire rack. Lift up on the foil handles to remove from the pan. Cut into 12 bars.

# Mango Bread Pudding

Mexican mangoes are plentiful in American markets from late spring through early summer. Depending on where you buy them, they can be downright cheap—a real bargain when you consider the mango's luxuriously fragrant flavor, like a peach on a tropical vacation. Bread puddings are a favorite Mexican dessert, and this one has a surprise layer of sliced mangoes on the bottom.

8 CUPS 1-INCH CUBES OF DAY-OLD FRENCH BREAD,
    WITH CRUSTS (ABOUT 12 OUNCES)
6 CUPS MILK
½ CUP (1 STICK) UNSALTED BUTTER
2 CUPS FIRMLY PACKED LIGHT BROWN SUGAR

6 LARGE EGGS, AT ROOM TEMPERATURE
1 ½ TEASPOONS VANILLA EXTRACT
½ TEASPOON GROUND CINNAMON
4 RIPE MANGOES, PEELED AND CHOPPED INTO
    ¾-INCH CUBES (SEE BELOW)

**1.** Preheat the oven to 325°F (see opposite page). Lightly butter a 13 × 9-inch glass baking dish. (If the bread cubes aren't day old, dry them out without toasting by placing in the oven while it is preheating, 15 to 20 minutes. Stir the cubes occasionally and let them cool before making the pudding.)

**2.** In a large saucepan, heat the milk and butter over medium heat, stirring often to melt the butter, and watching to be sure it doesn't boil over. Stir in the brown sugar to dissolve. Remove from heat.

**3.** In a large bowl, whisk the eggs, vanilla, and cinnamon. Gradually whisk in the hot milk mixture. Add the bread cubes and stir. Let stand for about 15 minutes, stirring often so the bread cubes soak up the liquid evenly.

**4.** Spread the mangoes evenly in the bottom of the baking dish. Pour in the bread mixture and spread evenly. Place the baking dish in a larger dish and transfer to the oven. Pour enough hot water into the larger dish to come about 1 inch up the sides. Bake until a knife inserted in the center comes out clean, about 1½ hours. Let stand for at least 1 hour before serving warm, chilled, or at room temperature.

Preparing mangoes can be a mystery to some people, but once you learn how, it's easy. Lay a ripe mango (it should yield slightly to pressure when squeezed) on a work surface, plump side down. The mango pit is long and flat, and runs horizontally through the fruit. The trick is to cut the flesh away without hitting the pit. Using a sharp, thin-bladed knife, slice off the top third of the mango, cutting around the pit. Turn the mango over and slice off the other side. One piece at a time, using a large serving spoon, scoop out the mango flesh in one piece from the peel. Cut the mango sections lengthwise into ½-inch slices. As the cook's treat, you can nibble away the flesh clinging to the pit.

Slow cooking is the way to a great bread pudding. Use an oven thermometer to be sure your oven temperature doesn't rise above 325°F, as higher temperatures will curdle the eggs in the custard.

# Cherry-Almond Oven Pancake

This is a variation on the French *clafoutis,* an oven pancake with a wonderful custardlike texture. It is a popular dish there; not only is it delicious but the batter takes seconds to make in a blender. Serve it puffed and hot as it comes out of the oven, dusted with confectioners' sugar, or let it cool and serve with a scoop of vanilla ice cream.

1 POUND DARK SWEET CHERRIES, SUCH AS BING, PITTED

6 LARGE EGGS

1 CUP MILK

¾ CUP ALL-PURPOSE FLOUR

½ CUP GRANULATED SUGAR

½ TEASPOON VANILLA EXTRACT

¼ TEASPOON ALMOND EXTRACT

⅛ TEASPOON SALT

⅓ CUP SLICED ALMONDS

2 TABLESPOONS UNSALTED BUTTER, CUT INTO SMALL BITS

CONFECTIONERS' SUGAR, FOR DUSTING

**1.** Position a rack in the center of the oven and preheat to 400°F. Lightly butter a 10-inch pie plate. Spread the cherries evenly in the pie plate.

**2.** In a blender, process the eggs, milk, flour, sugar, vanilla and almond extracts, and salt until smooth. Pour the batter evenly over the cherries. Sprinkle with the almonds and dot with the butter.

**3.** Bake until the pancake is puffed and browned and a toothpick inserted in the center comes out clean, 25 to 30 minutes. Remove from the oven and dust with the confectioners' sugar. Serve hot, warm, or at room temperature.

# Peach and Butterscotch Pudding Parfaits

Pudding is so simple to make from scratch, I can't figure out why some people make it out of a box. Butterscotch pudding is delicious on its own, but layered with peaches, it becomes an extra-special treat.

¾ CUP FIRMLY PACKED DARK BROWN SUGAR

¼ CUP CORNSTARCH

3 CUPS MILK

4 LARGE EGG YOLKS

2 TABLESPOONS UNSALTED BUTTER

1½ TEASPOONS VANILLA EXTRACT

4 RIPE LARGE PEACHES, PEELED, PITTED, AND
    COARSELY CHOPPED (SEE BELOW)

SWEETENED WHIPPED CREAM, FOR TOPPING

**1.** Combine the brown sugar and cornstarch in a medium, heavy-bottomed saucepan. Gradually add the milk, whisking to dissolve the cornstarch. Stirring constantly over medium heat, cook until thickened and simmering, being sure to reach into the corners of the saucepan with the spoon.

**2.** In a small bowl, whisk the egg yolks. Gradually whisk 1 cup of the hot milk mixture into the yolks, then whisk into the saucepan. Stirring constantly, return to the simmer and cook for 2 minutes. Remove from the heat and stir in the butter and vanilla. Spoon into a medium bowl. Place a piece of plastic wrap directly on the surface of the pudding, and pierce a few times with the tip of a sharp knife to allow the steam to escape. Cool to room temperature. Refrigerate until chilled, at least 1 hour.

**3.** In 4 wineglasses or parfait glasses, layer the pudding and peaches. Top each parfait with whipped cream and serve chilled.

**Variation:**
If serving these parfaits to grown-ups, mix the peaches with 2 tablespoons bourbon or dark rum, cover, and refrigerate for 2 hours.

To peel peaches, bring a large pot of water to a boil over high heat. Drop the peaches into the boiling water and cook until the peel loosens, no more than 1 minute. (If the peel doesn't loosen in the boiling water, the peaches weren't ripe enough to begin with, and you may have to pare the skin off with a sharp knife.) Using a slotted spoon, transfer the peaches to a bowl of cold water and let stand for a couple of minutes. Drain, then peel the peaches with a sharp knife.

# Chocolate Almond Tiramisù

One of these days, I am going to put on a blindfold and see if I can really make tiramisù with my eyes closed. I smile condescendingly at more complicated versions—the dessert was developed by Venetian cooks as an afternoon snack (*tiramisù* means "pick-me-up"), and snacks are never complicated.

½ CUP (ABOUT 5 OUNCES) SLICED ALMONDS,
    BLANCHED OR NATURAL
ONE 17½-OUNCE CONTAINER MASCARPONE,
    AT ROOM TEMPERATURE (2 CUPS)
½ CUP CONFECTIONERS' SUGAR
1 CUP HEAVY CREAM, CHILLED
1 TEASPOON VANILLA EXTRACT

1½ CUPS COOL, BREWED ESPRESSO COFFEE, OR DISSOLVE
    1 TABLESPOON INSTANT ESPRESSO POWDER IN ¾ CUP BOILING
    WATER, THEN STIR IN ¾ CUP COLD WATER TO COOL QUICKLY
3 TABLESPOONS AMARETTO OR KAHLÚA LIQUEUR
ONE 7-OUNCE PACKAGE ITALIAN DRY LADYFINGERS
    (*SAVOIARDI*)
2 OUNCES HIGH-QUALITY BITTERSWEET CHOCOLATE,
    FINELY CHOPPED

**1.** Preheat the oven to 350°F. Place the almonds in a single layer on a large baking sheet. Bake, stirring often, until toasted and golden brown, 10 to 12 minutes. Cool completely.

**2.** In a medium bowl, work the mascarpone and confectioners' sugar with a rubber spatula until smooth. In a chilled medium bowl, beat the cream and vanilla until stiff, then fold into the mascarpone.

**3.** In a wide bowl, mix the espresso and Kahlúa. One at a time, briefly dip half of the ladyfingers into the espresso mixture (do not soak them), then arrange in a 13 × 9-inch dish, breaking the ladyfingers as needed to fit into the pan. Don't worry about any gaps. Spread with half of the mascarpone mixture. Dip and layer the remaining ladyfingers, and spread with the rest of the mascarpone. Sprinkle with the almonds and the chocolate. Tightly cover with plastic wrap and refrigerate for at least 4 hours or overnight. To serve, spoon into wine goblets or bowls.

# Late Harvest Wine Zabaglione with Figs and Raspberries

MAKES 4 SERVINGS

The lush flavors in this dessert were inspired by a dessert I enjoyed in Chile, where pounds of sliced figs were layered with a sweet wine custard, pressed, and sliced like a pie. In this country, figs can get pretty pricey (unless you have a fig tree in the backyard), so I made this delicious variation. Zabaglione is usually made with sweet marsala, but the apricot-honey flavors of late-harvest riesling are a great twist on tradition. Thanks to my friend Lidia Bastianich of New York's Felidia Restaurant, whose fine book, *La Cucina di Felidia*, includes many details about making a good zabaglione.

18 RIPE FIGS (ABOUT 1 PINT), CUT LENGTHWISE
    INTO QUARTERS

6 OUNCES FRESH RASPBERRIES

4 LARGE EGG YOLKS, AT ROOM TEMPERATURE

¼ CUP GRANULATED SUGAR

¼ CUP LATE-HARVEST RIESLING OR GEWÜRZTRAMINER,
    OR ICE WINE

**1.** Gently mix the figs and raspberries and divide among 4 large wineglasses. Set aside.

**2.** In medium heatproof bowl, whisk together the yolks, sugar, and wine. Place over a medium saucepan filled with 2 inches of simmering, not boiling, water. Do not let the bottom of the bowl touch the water.

**3.** Using a wire balloon whisk or an electric hand mixer set at medium speed, beat the yolk mixture until hot, thick, and fluffy, 3 to 5 minutes. Without delay (if the zabaglione stands in the hot bowl too long without being whisked, it could curdle), spoon over the fruit. Serve immediately.

# Tin Roof Ice Cream Sundaes with Jack Daniel's Hot Fudge Sauce

This is the kind of warm chocolate sauce that firms up into a chewy chocolate cap. If you prefer a more liquid sauce, substitute an additional 1/4 cup heavy cream for the butter.

**JACK DANIEL'S HOT FUDGE SAUCE**

1/4 CUP HEAVY CREAM

1/4 CUP (1/2 STICK) UNSALTED BUTTER

6 OUNCES SEMISWEET OR BITTERSWEET CHOCOLATE, FINELY CHOPPED

2 TABLESPOONS BOURBON, SUCH AS JACK DANIEL'S, OR BREWED STRONG COFFEE, OR ADDITIONAL HEAVY CREAM

1 TABLESPOON LIGHT CORN SYRUP OR HONEY

**TO COMPLETE THE RECIPE**

1 1/2 PINTS VANILLA ICE CREAM

1/2 CUP CRUSHED PEANUT BRITTLE (PLACE THE BRITTLE IN A PAPER BAG AND CRUSH UNDER A ROLLING PIN)

SWEETENED WHIPPED CREAM, OPTIONAL

**1.** To make the sauce, heat the cream and butter in a medium saucepan over low heat until simmering, stirring to melt the butter. Remove from the heat and add the chocolate. Let stand until the chocolate softens, about 3 minutes, then whisk until smooth. Whisk in the bourbon and corn syrup. (The sauce can be stored at room temperature for up to 4 hours. Reheat gently, if desired, in a double boiler over hot water, or in a microwave. Do not simmer.)

**2.** To serve, scoop equal amounts of the ice cream into serving bowls. Top with the sauce, then sprinkle with the peanut brittle and spoon on the optional whipped cream.

# Grilled Peach Sundaes with Amaretto Sauce

MAKES 6 SERVINGS

These grilled peaches couldn't be more scrumptious. Cooked in foil pouches, they make their own sauce for pouring over ice cream.

6 RIPE MEDIUM PEACHES, PEELED, PITTED, AND CUT INTO 8 WEDGES EACH (SEE PAGE 181)
¾ CUP FIRMLY PACKED LIGHT BROWN SUGAR
¾ CUP (1½ STICKS) UNSALTED BUTTER

¾ CUP DARK RUM, OR ¾ CUP CANNED PEACH NECTAR WITH ¼ TEASPOON ALMOND EXTRACT
1 QUART VANILLA ICE CREAM

**1.** Build a hot fire in an outdoor grill and let the coals burn down until covered with white ash and medium-low. You should be able to hold your hand directly over the coals for 4 to 5 seconds. If you are grilling the peaches after grilling a main course, the coals may be too cool. Add about 12 briquettes to the coals and let them ignite and burn for about 20 minutes and covered with white ashes before proceeding. (Or preheat a gas grill on high, then adjust to low.)

**2.** Tear off 6 pieces of aluminum foil, each about 12 inches square. Fold a foil square in half, and reopen. In the center of the foil square's bottom half, spoon 2 tablespoons each of the brown sugar and butter. Top with 8 peach wedges. Drizzle 2 tablespoons of rum over the peach package. (This way, the sugar soaks up the rum, and the rum won't run all over.) Fold the top half of the foil down to cover the peach, and tightly crimp the 3 open edges closed. Repeat with the remaining ingredients.

**3.** Place the foil packages on the grill and cover. Cook until the butter has melted and a sauce has formed, 5 to 8 minutes. You can open up the top of one packet with scissors to check. Cool slightly. To serve, spoon the ice cream into large chilled wine goblets or bowls. Using scissors, cut each packet open, pouring the contents over each serving of ice cream.

# Strawberry-Lemonade Granita

My friends will tell you, I'm not one for bombast (by Texan standards), but this is
one of the most refreshing desserts in the universe. If no one is looking, sprinkle each serving
with a healthy shot of tequila or dark rum.

2 PINTS FRESH STRAWBERRIES, RINSED AND
    STEMS REMOVED
¾ CUP PLUS 2 TABLESPOONS SUGAR

¾ CUP FRESH LEMON JUICE
1 CUP WATER

**1.** Place a metal 13 × 9-inch baking dish in the freezer and freeze until very cold, about 30 minutes.

**2.** In a food processor, puree the strawberries; you should have 2 cups. Add the sugar, lemon juice, and water to the food processor, and process until the sugar is dissolved. (If the mixture threatens to spill out of the food processor, do this in batches.) Pour into the cold pan and return to the freezer. Freeze until the strawberry mixture begins to freeze solid around the edges, about 1 hour, depending on your freezer's temperature.

**3.** Using a long metal spoon, scrape and stir the partially frozen mixture into the center of the pan. (Leave the spoon in the pan.) Freeze again until the mixture is partially frozen with ice crystals around the edges, about 1 more hour. Repeat the stirring procedure and return to the freezer. Freeze until the mixture is almost completely frozen into slushy ice crystals, about 1 more hour. Stir again and keep frozen until ready to serve, up to 2 hours.

**4.** Break up the ice crystals and spoon into ice-cold glasses (I like martini glasses). Serve immediately.

# mail-order sources

**THE EL PASO CHILE COMPANY**
909 Texas Avenue
El Paso, TX 79901
(915) 544-3434

**BUENO FOODS**
2001 4th Street SW
Albuquerque, NM 87102
(505) 243-2722

**CASADOS FARMS**
P.O. Box 852
San Juan Pueblo, NM 87566
(505) 852-2433

**COYOTE CAFÉ GENERAL STORE**
132 West Water Street
Santa Fe, NM 87501
(800) 866-HOWL

# INDEX

spinach:
    ginger-sesame, 153
    -stuffed tomatoes, 156
squash:
    acorn, Caribbean beef and kale
      soup, 23
    two-, sauté with oregano and
      lemon, 154
    winter, vegetable and poblano
      stew, 124
strawberry(ies):
    blueberry scone-cake with,
      170–171
    -lemonade granita, 186
stuffing, cranberry-sausage, for
    crown roast of pork and
      bourbon gravy, 94–95
sundaes:
    grilled peach, with amaretto
      sauce, 185
    tin roof ice cream, with Jack
      Daniel's hot fudge sauce,
      184

## T

tomato(es):
    black, yellow, and red salad with
      lime vinaigrette, 15
    and bread salad, rosemary
      chicken on, 64
    and corn risotto,
      120–121

    grilled beefsteak, with basil oil,
      155
    *olivada,* for mozzarella
      quesadillas, 122–123
    spinach-stuffed, 156
    Zinfandel-sauce, for orzo-
      stuffed peppers, 118
tortilla soup, my, 26–27
tuna:
    au poivre with port sauce, 53
    Sicilian spaghetti with eggplant
      and, 141
    and zucchini kebabs with
      orange-tarragon marinade, 52
turkey:
    classic, pot pie with scallion
      biscuit topping, 80–81
    roulades with jalapeño jack and
      prosciutto, 79

## V

veal and artichoke stew with
    gremolata, 110–111
vegetable:
    and poblano stew, 124
    soup, green, with cheese
      gnocchi, 35

## W

white bean and garlic soup with
    grilled sausage, 36–37

wine:
    cooking with, 68–69, 75, 137
    late harvest, zabaglione with figs
      and raspberries, 183
    orzo-stuffed peppers with
      Zinfandel-tomato sauce,
      118

## Y

yams, oven-roasted, chile-kissed,
    157–158
yogurt marinade, Mediterranean,
    for grilled leg of lamb,
      106–107

## Z

zabaglione, late harvest wine, with
    figs and raspberries, 183
zucchini:
    grilled, with balsamic sage
      vinaigrette, 12
    and orange pound cake,
      163
    and rice casserole, 127
    roast vegetable and provolone
      pizza, 119
    and tuna kebabs with orange-
      tarragon marinade,
      52
    two-squash sauté with oregano
      and lemon, 154